CAMBRIDGE LIBRAF

Books of enduring sch

Literary studies

This series provides a high-quality selection of early printings of literary works, textual editions, anthologies and literary criticism which are of lasting scholarly interest. Ranging from Old English to Shakespeare to early twentieth-century work from around the world, these books offer a valuable resource for scholars in reception history, textual editing, and literary studies.

A Chapter in the Early Life of Shakespeare

In this charming and thought-provoking 1926 volume, Arthur Gray, Master of Jesus College, Cambridge from 1912 to 1940, explored the possibility that William Shakespeare spent his formative years at Polesworth Hall in the Forest of Arden, perhaps serving as a page boy. The Forest of Arden once stretched from just north of Stratford-upon-Avon to Tamworth, and covered what is now Birmingham; Polesworth, near Tamworth, was the home of Sir Henry Goodere and the centre of the famed 'Polesworth Circle'. This splendid focus of creative and cultural activity would have offered the young William exposure to the finest minds, a wonderful education and valuable introductions. Sir Henry, who evidently knew John Shakespeare in Stratford, was certainly patron of many young writers and musicians, including the eminent Elizabethan poet, Michael Drayton. If Gray is correct, Drayton would have been a contemporary of Shakespeare's at Polesworth.

Cambridge University Press has long been a pioneer in the reissuing of out-of-print titles from its own backlist, producing digital reprints of books that are still sought after by scholars and students but could not be reprinted economically using traditional technology. The Cambridge Library Collection extends this activity to a wider range of books which are still of importance to researchers and professionals, either for the source material they contain, or as landmarks in the history of their academic discipline.

Drawing from the world-renowned collections in the Cambridge University Library, and guided by the advice of experts in each subject area, Cambridge University Press is using state-of-the-art scanning machines in its own Printing House to capture the content of each book selected for inclusion. The files are processed to give a consistently clear, crisp image, and the books finished to the high quality standard for which the Press is recognised around the world. The latest print-on-demand technology ensures that the books will remain available indefinitely, and that orders for single or multiple copies can quickly be supplied.

The Cambridge Library Collection will bring back to life books of enduring scholarly value across a wide range of disciplines in the humanities and social sciences and in science and technology.

A Chapter in the Early
Life of Shakespeare

Polesworth in Arden

ARTHUR GRAY

CAMBRIDGE
UNIVERSITY PRESS

CAMBRIDGE UNIVERSITY PRESS

Cambridge New York Melbourne Madrid Cape Town Singapore São Paolo Delhi

Published in the United States of America by Cambridge University Press, New York

www.cambridge.org
Information on this title: www.cambridge.org/9781108005579

This edition first published 1926
This digitally printed version 2009

ISBN 978-1-108-00557-9

A CHAPTER
IN THE EARLY LIFE
OF SHAKESPEARE

CAMBRIDGE
UNIVERSITY PRESS

LONDON: Fetter Lane

New York
The Macmillan Co.

Bombay, Calcutta and Madras
Macmillan and Co., Ltd.

Toronto
The Macmillan Co. of Canada, Ltd.

Tokyo
Maruzen-Kabushiki-Kaisha

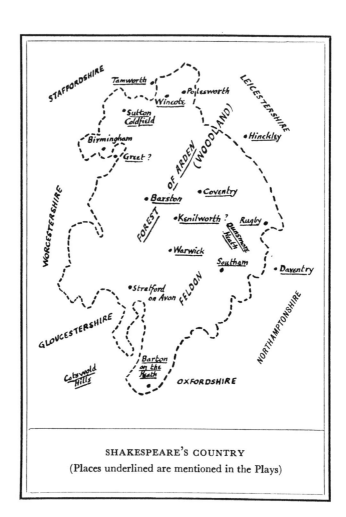

Staffordshire

Tamworth • • Poilesworth
Wincote •

• Sutton Coldfield

Leicestershire

Birmingham •

• Hinckley

• Greet ?

FOREST OF ARDEN (WOODLAND)

Worcestershire

• Barston

• Coventry

• Kenilworth ? • Rugby

Dunsmore Heath

• Warwick

Southam

• Daventry

FELDON

• Stratford on Avon

Gloucestershire

Northamptonshire

Cotswold Hills

Barton on the Heath

Oxfordshire

SHAKESPEARE'S COUNTRY

(Places underlined are mentioned in the Plays)

A CHAPTER
IN THE EARLY LIFE
OF
SHAKESPEARE

POLESWORTH
IN ARDEN

BY
ARTHUR GRAY, M.A.
Master of Jesus College
Cambridge

CAMBRIDGE
at the University Press
MCMXXVI

VETULAE MEAE

A·H·G

CONTENTS

ILLUSTRATIONS

'*Horatio.* 'Twere to consider too curiously, to consider so.
Hamlet. No, faith, not a jot: but to follow with modesty
   enough and likelihood to lead it.'

In describing this Essay as A Chapter in the Early
Life of Shakespeare, I am conscious that I may be
charged with some presumption as well as that
'curiosity' which is deprecated by Horatio. I do
not claim for proven a contention which rests on
hypothesis, however buttressed with circumstance.
With Hamlet I follow with modesty where likelihood leads.

   It cannot be a matter indifferent to us to trace
the natural stages which brought the Stratford boy
to the heights of his transfiguration. The blank
period of Shakespeare's youth can only be filled
with material which is largely conjectural. But
conjecture must not surpass the limits of the
humanly credible, and it must begin with no
postulates or undocumented assumptions. If it be
assumed that Shakespeare stood apart from all the
conditions which govern the rest of humanity, and
that in the preparation for his life's work he neither
had nor required the helps and suggestions without
which the celestial fire cannot in other men be
fanned into flame, then *cadit quaestio.* If the
ordinarily accepted tradition of his stunted education, mean surroundings and coarse occupation at
Stratford be an article of orthodox belief, then
I should be fain to accept the Baconian faith, or

profess myself, with Sir George Greenwood, a pure agnostic. Convinced as I am that in neither position is salvation to be found, I advance a new hypothesis which may meet the objections raised by either heretical school to the not unreasonable belief that Shakespeare—spell his name as we will —wrote Shakespeare's Works.

I plead for common sense, for some evidence of fact and for the elimination of doubtfully 'doubt-less' guesswork. Not without cause Baconians and Greenwoodians are afflicted and scandalised by the demands on which the Stratford faith insists. So far as it relates to Shakespeare's life before his emergence on the London stage, that creed rests on no evidence other than gossip—ignorant, confused, contradictory, and gathered a century or more after the time to which it relates. If Shakespeare be allowed to speak for himself he will tell us a good deal about Warwickshire—nothing about Stratford, nothing definite about any place near it—and, unconsciously, something about the conditions of his early life.

Of Shakespeare, poet and dramatist, Stratford has precisely nothing to say. All Warwickshire sings of him: his verses hang on every tree in Arden. Only Stratford is deaf to that music, and dumb for any echoes of its own. Bethlehem and the sepulchre door. 'Remember how he *spake* unto you.' No, Stratford remembers only the cradle and the grave. Standing in its glorious church, where the monument is neighboured and out-rivalled by

the pomp of the Clopton chapel, I say to myself,
'He made his grave with the rich in his death,
because there was no deceit in his mouth.' But, as
was said to the first pilgrims at a holier tomb, I add,
'He is not here.'

But if not at the shrine which modern piety has
enriched and hallowed to his memory, what
quarter, it will be asked, has better claim to have
been tenanted by him in his growing years, and
to have had place in his memory in the time of his
productivity? To destroy an old faith is not enough,
unless a better way of believing is offered in its
room. It is possible that many devout Stratfordians
may welcome a creed which needs no artificial
apologies. To substitute such a creed is the aim of
this Essay. *Hoc opus, hic labor est.* I do not claim
for my thesis that it is beyond the range of critical
sharpshooters. I do claim for it that it is reasonable
and that it offers a view of Shakespeare's education
which obeys the laws of perspective. Further investigation in a field which I have only partially
explored may bring to light evidence in its verifica-
tion.

§ 2 THE MARLOWE FICTION

Dr Hotson's book, *The Death of Marlowe* (1925), is
a monument of patient research resulting in a
surprising discovery. It is equally remarkable as
proving the worthlessness of gossiping tales, even
when they are concerned with nearly contemporary

matters, and of the inferences which in later times have been piled on such unsubstantial foundations.

Christopher Marlowe unquestionably died by a dagger-stroke on May 30, 1593. The circumstances of his death were utilised by contemporary precisians to illustrate their homilies on the evils of 'atheism' and debauchery. The first account appears in Thomas Beard's *Theatre of God's Iudgements*, printed in 1597. Omitting prolix and pious scurrilities, we learn from it that the fray which resulted in Marlowe's death happened 'in London streets.' Francis Meres, in his *Palladis Tamia* (1598), citing Beard's authority, amplifies the details: Christopher Marlowe 'was stabd to death by a bawdy serving man, a rivall of his in lewde love.' In 1600, William Vaughan had a variation of the story: the scene of the fatality is laid by him at 'Detford, a little village about three miles distant from London,' the slayer is 'one named Ingram,' and the two were playing 'at tables' just before the quarrel: the 'lewde love' disappears in his version. Some eighty years after the event comes John Aubrey—one of the first remembrancers of Shakespeare—with the amazing statement that Ben Jonson 'killed Mr Marlow, the poet, on Bunhill, coming from the Green Curtain playhouse.' Lastly, Anthony à Wood, in 1691, adds the improving touches that 'Marlowe was deeply in love with a certain Woman,' and that his rival was 'fitter to be a Pimp.' In 1820 an antiquary elicited from the register of Deptford church an entry of Marlowe's

The Marlowe Fiction

burial on June 1, 1593, in which the slayer's name was read as 'Francis Archer.' With the substitution of Archer's name for Ingram's every writer, until the other day, implicitly accepted the story, only reconciling the discrepancies in its various versions and adding 'improvements' such as lent themselves to their interpretation of it. According to one of them the slayer was Francis Ingram, and he is variously described as a servant maintained by Marlowe, a lackey, a scullion, and so forth. According to another, Marlowe was in love with a woman described in language 'which we cannot bring ourselves to repeat': Ingram plots to meet this 'stolen lady-love' at a low-class tavern in Deptford, and thence comes the trouble.

Finally comes Dr Hotson to sweep away all these cobwebs of hearsay and speculation. He goes to Deptford and finds that the slayer's name is unmistakably written Francis Ffrezer. He discovers the return of the Coroner's inquisition, in which it is given as Ingram Ffrysar. He discovers further that Ffrysar is no serving man, but, whatever his character, is nominated 'generosus,' and he turns out to be a person of some social position. The meeting place is not in London streets, but at a rural inn at Deptford, which is of sufficient consequence to have a garden wherein Marlowe and Ffrysar walk. There is no woman in the case: the affray is about a dispute in the reckoning. The findings of the Coroner's jury bring out with minute precision all the circumstances of the story.

The Marlowe Fiction

Contrast the beginnings and the developments of this Marlowe legend with the fictions about the early life of Shakespeare at Stratford. In the former case we have Beard's bald statement, which was in print within four years from the date of the occurrences. Within a year Meres added a fiction of his own devising, and three years later Vaughan furnishes an independent version conflicting with the previous tales. And Aubrey, whom Sir Sidney Lee calls 'Shakespeare's first biographer'—what is to be said of his wild invention? In the nineteenth century a torrent of guess-work fills the vacancies unoccupied in the earlier narratives.

Now take the Stratford legend. Shakespeare had been in his grave for two generations before anybody thought of jotting down reminiscences of him. The earliest anecdotist confesses that he knew nothing of Shakespeare's plays. Those who followed him in the seventeenth century are convicted of gross blunders, mis-statements and contradictions. They affect to know what had happened, a century before their time, to an obscure youth, but of the great man who died in their town half a century later they have nothing whatever to say. The first printed account of Shakespeare's life appeared ninety-three years after his death, when his last descendant was long dead, and even the house in which he lived and died had been destroyed*. So

* Fuller, who died in 1661 and whose *Worthies of Warwickshire* was published in 1662, supplies no facts in the life of Shakespeare.

The Marlowe Fiction

far as it deals with recorded fact, Rowe's narrative is honest enough: but fact had less attraction for Rowe and his age than its elegant presentation, and episode, such as that of the deer-stealing, needed no close investigation of evidences to justify its introduction in an otherwise bare recital. Whatever his fault in that matter, nineteenth-century 'criticism' far outwent him in its suggestion that the unproved is doubtless or certainly true, and the assumption that Shakespeare's genius was exempt from the laws that operate in the case of lesser men has fostered in biographers the notion that in his case the work of fancy is believable *quia impossibile*.

Such is not the way to fill the void places in Shakespeare's career before the rising of his star in 1593. There is but one way—to let Shakespeare reveal himself in unconscious reminiscence of the conditions of his early life, and to exclude such supposed direct references as he expressly tells us are opposed to the principles of his art. If to the evidence of his word we can add such facts as without improbability may be brought into relation with that evidence, we shall stand on, not secure, but safer ground. And if the facts and that evidence can be wrought into a continuous clue, I think that it may be claimed that we are in a way to emerge into daylight. That the day has yet come I am far from asserting, but with better knowledge it may come.

7

The Greenwood Theory

Before I proceed to the discussion of the sources of
the Stratford Legend I am drawn into a bypath
by the attractive and ably argued theory of Sir G. G.
Greenwood that the Plays and Poems of 'Shakespeare' were not the work of the man who wrote
his name 'Shakspere,' who was born and died at
Stratford, and was merely a popular actor. Inasmuch as the actor was a Warwickshire man and
the Plays are full of Warwickshire, the divagation
is not so irrelevant as at first view it may seem.

Sir George Greenwood is by no means out to
substitute an impossible Bacon for an actual but
unwriting Shakespeare. In one contention I hold
that, for all that the Orthodox have alleged against
it, he is signally right. I agree with him that
William Shakespeare, as he figures in the Stratford
Apocrypha, was not, and could not be, the William
Shakespeare who wrote the Plays and Poems.

But, if not Bacon, then Who? Sir George offers
us only an unknown and neuter *Tertium Quid*. What
I want, and what in reason everybody demands, is
a *Tertius Quis*. Can we realise no more of the
author of *Hamlet* and *Lear* than we do of the something called Homer? In the dual Shakspere-
Shakespeare of his begetting, Sir George, by not
confounding the persons but dividing their sub-
stance, imperils my faith in human individuality.
I confess myself so far an orthodox Shakespearean
that I must clothe his unessential dramatist in some

8

The Greenwood Theory

likeness of a man. Somewhere in this breathing world there lived a man, whose name may or may not have been Shakespeare, but who wrote plays, which were 'Shakespeare's Works.'

To follow and discuss the long train of Sir George's argument* that 'Shakspere,' the actor, was not the same man as 'Shakespeare' of the Works is beside my purpose, which is to suggest a simple way of identifying 'the rustic' with the only man whom it is worth our while to call Shakespeare—the man whose name, so spelt, is prefixed to most that in quarto or folio passed for Shakespeare with his contemporaries. I cannot convince myself that 'Shakespeare,' or 'Shake-speare,' was merely a *nom de plume*, veiling another writer. That the Stratford man wrote his name 'Shakspere' counts for little. The name, a common one in Warwickshire, was written in a great variety of ways, and though it cannot be proved that the dramatist's kinsfolk ever wrote it 'Shakespeare,' the London printers showed no uniformity in spelling it 'Shakespeare,' or 'Shake-speare,' in the titles which were prefixed to the quartos published while the author was alive. Briefly, I cannot believe that Jonson, who knew the actor Shakspere, was mistaken in crediting him with the authorship of Shakespeare's plays; I cannot doubt that his 'Star of Poets' was indeed the 'Swan of Avon'; I cannot

* Sir G. G. Greenwood, *The Shakespeare Problem Re-stated* (1908), *In Re Shakespeare, Beeching and Greenwood* (1909), *Is there a Shakespeare Problem?* (1916), *Shakespeare and a Tertium Quid* (1923).

9

doubt the statement of Heminge and Condell that they 'received from him (*i.e.* the dramatist) his papers with scarse a blot,' a statement accepted as true by Jonson. Some of the plays which they included in the First Folio were unquestionably printed from quarto texts, but others from stage copies in Shakespeare's writing, and it is hard to believe that they were unacquainted with the handwriting of their 'Friend and Fellow,' the actor.

It would be easy to multiply evidences of the identity of the player with the playwright. I content myself with mentioning one fact: I shall come back to it later. By his contemporaries and the generation next succeeding them the dramatist was constantly associated with Warwickshire. The connection, no doubt, was suggested by the fact that he spent his last years at Stratford, and that there he died and was commemorated by the monument in the church. Jonson's 'Swan of Avon' and Milton's 'native wood-notes' may very well imply no more than this. Sir Aston Cokain, in verses addressed to Dugdale 'upon his *Warwickshire Illustrated*' (1658), expresses the pride which he, a Warwickshire man, had in his famous fellow-countyman:

> 'Now, *Stratford* upon *Avon*, we would choose
> Thy gentle and ingenuous *Shakespeare* Muse
> (Were he among the living yet) to raise
> T'our Antiquaries merit some just praise.

.   .   .   .   .

The Greenwood Theory

Our Warwickshire the Heart of England is,
As you most evidently have prov'd by this,
Having it with more spirit dignifi'd
Then all our *English* Counties are beside.'

Conversely, Shakespeare pays notable tribute to the qualities of the men of Warwickshire,

'Not mutinous in peace, yet bold in war.'
Henry VI, C, iv, 8. 10.

But the best evidence of the dramatist's county patriotism comes from what he says, in quite an incidental way, about Warwickshire localities, many of them petty places whose names and existence could only be known to a man native to the region and widely travelled in it. Outside London there is no part of England with which Shakespeare's contemporaries in drama show any familiarity. With him and his Warwickshire neighbour, Drayton, begins regional poetry, taken up long afterwards by the Romanticists. And not only are the names familiar as household words in Shakespeare's mouth: the breath of Warwickshire woodlands is in *Venus and Adonis*, *Love's Labour's Lost* and *Midsummer Night's Dream*, and Arden, for all its exotic assemblage of trees and beasts, is as surely a transfiguration of the Arden of Shakespeare's knowledge as it is certain that the pastorals of Jonson, Fletcher and Milton have nothing in them to recall Sherwood, Thessaly or Shropshire. Was it Bacon of Norfolk who so delighted himself in Warwickshire scenes and people? Or was it Fulke Greville, a Warwickshire man and a dramatist,

The Greenwood Theory

though his scene is anywhere but in England? Failing him, I can think of no likelier claimant for the local laureateship than the Stratford actor.

But then the dramatist known to us as Shakespeare never mentions Stratford on the Avon: except the Cotswold Hills he mentions no place particularly near Stratford. True, he does allude to the Lucy coat of arms, the dozen white luces, visible to all Stratford folk at Charlecote Hall: but perversely he makes Shallow a Gloucestershire justice. Shall we say that the man who could blunder in a matter so evident to every Stratford schoolboy, who talked of Coventry, Sutton Coldfield and less likely places in the shire, to the neglect of the town of his nativity and abode, was anyone rather than Stratford William*?

Of that more presently.

* Nobody seriously disputes that Shakespeare was born at Stratford, and I am not at all disposed to deny that he was familiar with the neighbourhood during some part of his boyhood and early married life. I make no doubt that the 'dozen white luces' in Shallow's coat of arms is a genuine allusion to the Lucy shield prominently displayed on the porch of Charlecote Hall (built *c.* 1558). I am the more led to think so by a passage in which I detect another allusion (not, I think, hitherto observed) to this same porch. In *Love's Labour's Lost* (v, 2) Costard says to Sir Nathaniel, 'Your lion that holds his pole-axe, sitting on a close-stool, will be given to Ajax.' The attitude of the two sitting lions on the balustrade of the porch, each upholding a pole-axe, has a ludicrous resemblance to the lion of Costard's description. But the jest of 'luces-louses' was of venerable antiquity when *Merry Wives* was written, and in Holinshed's version there is no reference to Lucy or Charlecote.

12

The Stratford Legend

Well, what are the ascertained and documented facts which connect Shakespeare with Stratford? Excluding transactions in and after 1597, when he was thirty-three, concerning the acquisition of property in the town or near it, they are meagre in the last degree. Except his will, no line in any official record substantiates his identity with the William of London and the stage. We do know that a certain William, son of John Shakespeare, was baptised in Stratford church on April 26, 1564, and it is reasonable to suppose that he was the same William who had children baptised in the same church in 1583 and 1585, and who was buried there on April 25, 1616. The father, John, was presumably the tradesman of that name who held a succession of municipal offices in the borough, ending with that of High Bailiff in 1568. John's wife, Mary, was apparently of the stock of the Ardens, a family of some standing in the county. Of William's education in boyhood and occupation in youth there is no vestige of evidence. He apparently married, but no record of the place or date of the ceremony exists. There is some question whether his wife's maiden name was Agnes or Anne Hathaway or Anne Whateley, and there is no conclusive evidence that she was born or lived at Shottery. After the birth of his twin children in February 1585, Stratford completely loses sight of him. From that time, until his appearance in

13

The Stratford Legend

London, seven years later, there is not a whisper of his whereabouts or occupation. We do not know when he left Stratford or when he returned to live there. We do not know whether his wife and children accompanied or followed him to London. We do not know the circumstances which induced him to go thither, how he lived in those silent London years, what brought him into contact with players, or how the Stratford tradesman's son came into intimate acquaintance with the Right Honourable the Earl of Southampton.

On the slight substructure of the Stratford records a monstrous fabric of fable, gossip, inference and pure surmise has been raised. 'Possibly' and 'perhaps' merge into 'clearly' and 'doubtless' in matters where the business of the biographer is to doubt or to deny. Among the 'Lives' of Shakespeare the *Outlines* of Halliwell-Phillipps may be preferred as giving the sources of assertions and making a somewhat judicial distinction between the more and the less probable. I turn to the Index in his second volume under the heading *Shakespeare, William*. Among others I find the following references: 'Enters the grammar-school,' 'Removed prematurely from school in order that he might assist his father in the wool business,' 'Apprenticed to a butcher,' 'The deer-stealing escapade,' 'His consequent departure from Stratford for London,' 'Temporary return to Stratford after the danger from the Lucy prosecution had subsided.' For all these statements there is no foundation of fact, and most of them have no probability to recommend them. Worse than that, they remove the real Shakespeare from us and make him incomprehensible, a portent. Portent-belief is only possible if the portents happened long ago and in conditions unknown. It is our ill fortune that we look on Shakespeare over an empty gulf of three centuries. So the legend that began in uncritical fable has come to be a matter of faith, and it is taken for axiom that, *temp.* Elizabeth, dunghill curs might confront the Helicons, and of uninstructed instinct scale their heights.

In his last years, when he lived in their midst, and for half a century after his death the Stratford folk showed no more interest in Shakespeare than in any other man who had made money and lived in a good house in their town. Allowing for the fertility of 'reminiscence' in uneducated minds there needs no surprise that the boy, William, was remembered when the man of the New Place was completely forgotten. Nobody took any note of the man's sayings or doings. It is unlikely that in that bookless town anybody had read his plays, not very probable that anybody had seen him on the London stage. His dealings in malt, tithes and the matter of enclosure were of much nearer concern to his fellow-burghers. The first Stratfordian who has left any notes of him (date between 1661 and 1663), John Ward, vicar of the parish, was alive to the fact that 'he had an allowance so large that he spent at the rate of £1000 a year'—a statement

15

The Stratford Legend

as questionable as that 'in his elder days he livd at Stratford and supplied the stage with two plays every year,' and that he 'died of a feavour' after a merry meeting with Drayton and Ben Jonson. As he makes a memorandum 'to peruse Shakespeare's plays and be versed in them, that I may not be ignorant of them,' it would seem that he had small or no acquaintance with them when he wrote. Perhaps Dugdale's reference to Shakespeare in his *Warwickshire* (1656) was bringing early enthusiasts to the shrine, and by their curiosity the worthy parson's attention was distracted from good books to plays.

John Aubrey wrote his notes on Shakespeare at some time later than 1680. He does not say that he had visited Stratford, but perhaps from neighbours there he picked up some old wives' tales. On such information he gathered that William's father was a butcher, and that Shakespeare himself had 'exercised his father's trade.' The story is something discredited by the circumstance that he heard of another butcher's boy of Stratford, a nameless 'co-etanean' of Shakespeare and in local opinion 'not at all inferior to him for a naturall witt, but dyed young.' The coincidence of two rivals in butchery and wit suggests a doubt whether the talent of the 'co-etanean' in the heroical slaughter of calves was not mistakenly transferred by the gossips to the poet*. Be that as it may, since Aubrey

* If it were not the case—as it is—that Aubrey knew next to nothing of Shakespeare's plays, I should guess that some dim

16

The Stratford Legend

says (possibly correctly) that Drayton too was a butcher's son, it must seem a curious coincidence that two Warwickshire butchers had sons who contemporaneously exchanged their fathers' mystery for the trade of poet. Aubrey is dreadfully to seek when it comes to any knowledge of Shakespeare's writings. Yet in his 'skimble skamble stuff' there is one grain of information which has some verisimilitude, and which he got from 'old Mr Beeston, whom Mr John Dryden calls the chronicle of the stage' and who died 'about Bartholomew tyde, 1682.' From him Aubrey derived the statement: 'Though, as Ben Jonson says of him that he had but little Latine and lesse Greek, he understood Latine pretty well, for he had been in his younger days a schoolmaster in the countrey.' When Aubrey wrote, no more trustworthy authority could be cited than William Beeston, actor and son of an actor contemporary with Shakespeare. 'Fancy Will Shakespeare a country pedagogue!' cries Sir George Greenwood. Fancy John Milton a pedagogue! Yet for seven years he kept a private school in London. Though we do well to doubt the wool- or butcher-business of Stratford myth, on the other hand there is no sense in super-humanising the Will of, let us say, 1583 to 1585. Poets may have

reminiscence of the part of Julius Caesar played by Polonius and of Hamlet's comment on 'calf-killing' thereon crossed his mind. I am even surprised that so obvious a suggestion has not been worked up by 'criticism' into an identification of Shakespeare with Brutus. The parallel is at least as good as that of Shakespeare-Falstaff.

us to believe that their youth is fostered on Hybla honey and milk of Paradise: hard crusts and broken meat are as often their prosaic diet. I fancy nothing is more probable than that a married youth, with a growing family and parents who could give him no help, should have taken to the honourable profession which rather later was exercised by Philemon Holland at Coventry. But then the humblest usher in a country school must have had an ampler education than Will had got from Stratford school, which, according to the Stratfordians, he left for his father's business at the age of thirteen.

A Gloucestershire parson, William Fulman, who died in 1688 and was something of an antiquarian, left a few manuscript notes about Shakespeare which add nothing to our knowledge. Unhappily, the book containing them came into the possession of another Gloucestershire parson, Richard Davies, who, at a date before 1708, intercalated some observations of his own. The measure of his folly and ignorance, alike of Shakespeare and heraldry, is given in his remarks: 'Much given to all unluckinesse in stealing venison and rabbits, particularly from Sr . . . Lucy, who had him oft whipt and sometimes imprisoned, and at last made him fly his native country to his great advancement: but his revenge was so great that he is his Justice Clodpate, and calls him a great man, and that in allusion to his name bore three lowses rampant for his arms: he dyed a papist.' It is worth remembering that, about the time when this was written, there was a similar legend that Milton had been 'whipt' (at Cambridge) and that he too died a papist. The genesis of the deer-stealing episode shall be dealt with presently. Stratfordians treat it as independent of Betterton's story. It is based on an identification of Sir Thomas Lucy with Justice Shallow, suggested by the opening lines of *Merry Wives*, a play which the parson had not read, and no Stratford parishioner is likely to have read. I make no question that Betterton was the source of the fiction.

Betterton, who died in 1710 at the age of something like 75, visited Stratford at an uncertain date —probably in the last quarter of the seventeenth century. It is unfortunate that we know no more of his researches there than is told by Rowe in the 'Account of the Life of Shakespeare' which he printed with his edition of the Plays, issued in 1709. It does not seem that Rowe made any independent enquiries. Betterton's information was drawn mainly from 'the register and publick writings relating to that town' (*i.e.* Stratford), which he cites with accuracy. Unfortunately he, like more recent writers of 'Lives,' in the deficiency of these sources added inferences which are of questionable value. He reports that John Shakespeare was 'a considerable dealer in wool,' and adds that he had so many children—he puts the number at *ten*— 'that he could give him (Shakespeare) no better education than his own employment.' 'He had bred him, 'tis true, for some time at a free school'—

The Stratford Legend

Rowe does not say that it was Stratford school—
'where 'tis probable that he acquired that little
Latin he was master of: but the narrowness of his
circumstances and the want of his assistance at
home forc'd his father to withdraw him from
thence, and unhappily prevented his further proficiency in that language. Upon his leaving school
he seems to have given intirely into that way of
living which his father propos'd to him: and in
order to settle in the world after a family manner,
he thought fit to marry while he was yet very
young'—a 'settlement,' surely, remarkable in a
penniless apprentice. 'In this kind of settlement he
continu'd for some time, 'till an extravagance that
he was guilty of forc'd him both out of his country
and that way of living that he had taken up. . . .
He had, by a misfortune common enough to young
fellows, fallen into ill company; and amongst them,
some that made a frequent practice of deer-
stealing engag'd him with them more than once
in robbing a park that belong'd to Sir Thomas
Lucy of Cherlecot, near Stratford. For this he was
prosecuted by that gentleman, as he thought,
somewhat too severely; and in order to revenge
that ill usage, he made a ballad upon him. And
tho' this, probably the first essay of his poetry, be
lost, yet it is said to have been so very bitter that
it redoubled the prosecution against him to that
degree, that he was oblig'd to leave his business
and family in Warwickshire for some time, and
shelter himself in London.'

The Stratford Legend

Speaking of the *Merry Wives*, Rowe adds, 'He has given him' (Justice Shallow) 'very near the same coat of arms which Dugdale in his Antiquities of that county' (Warwick) 'describes for a family there, and makes the Welsh parson descant very pleasantly upon 'em.' It is easy to see how the Lucy connection was suggested. Betterton was a Shakespeare enthusiast. Among the parts which he played was that of Falstaff. He wrote for the stage 'A Sequel of *Henry IV* with the Humours of Sir John Falstaffe and Justice Shallow.' His visit to Stratford was, no doubt, prompted by the account and picture of Shakespeare's monument given in Dugdale's book, and the same book depicts and describes the Lucy arms at Charlecote. The Lucy and the Shallow coat being practically identical, what inference more natural than that Shallow dramatically *is* Lucy? Argal, somebody stole Sir Thomas Lucy's deer, and by the same reasoning Falstaff-Shakespeare was that somebody, and was prosecuted, and fled from justice, and after brooding over the matter for some ten years avenged himself by an absurd stage caricature of his enemy, and the London (or Windsor) audience perfectly understood the joke, and wept trickling tears of mirth over the ridiculous counterfeit of the Warwickshire knight, as Mistress Quickly did at a similar piece of play-acting, 'O Jesu, this is excellent sport 'i faith.'

Is it necessary to ravel out this string of inconsequences? Alas, it is. Before the probable or more possible can find place for itself the ground must be cleared of the impossible and absurd, and the Charlecote legend is a main article of the Stratford faith. Sir Walter Raleigh accepts it as 'perfectly credible.' Halliwell-Phillipps says that it 'cannot admit of a doubt.' Sir Sidney Lee says that the identity of Shallow and Sir Thomas Lucy is 'fully established.' Now putting aside the not irrelevant fact that Sir Thomas Lucy had no deer-park at Charlecote or anywhere else, let us ask how Shakespeare came to drag this incident by head and ears into *Merry Wives*, and immediately to drop it. Shallow is of no consequence in the play; the mantle of his foolishness has fallen on Slender. 'I have lived fourscore years and upwards. I have never heard a man of his place, gravity and learning so wide of his respect'—is not that a lamentable descent to commonplace good sense*? The play, of course, is written for a command performance, and Shallow must have his part in it as well as Falstaff. By what device is he to be brought to Windsor? A Star Chamber suit, in which Falstaff is to be defendant, is the thin excuse. Before the scene is well through *exeunt* Shakespeare and Sir Thomas Lucy to share Master Page's venison pasty and drink down all unkindness. An odd 'revenge.' 'Call you this railing?'

---

* Shallow being aged upwards of eighty, it is perhaps worth observation that Lucy (b. 1532) was not more than fifty-three at the time of the supposed deer-stealing business. Falstaff, on the evidence of *Henry IV*, Part II, being a 'co-etanean' of Shallow, at what patriarchal age had the Falstaff-Shakespeare of *Merry Wives* arrived? But Shakespeare does not trouble himself about consistency.

Does Shakespeare Rail?

§ 5 DOES SHAKESPEARE RAIL?

Is it not a total misunderstanding of Shakespeare's character and the canons of his art to suppose that he 'rails'? If in Shallow he permits himself to gibbet Lucy, it is the only example of personal satire—I might add, of personal reminiscence— that can be reasonably detected in his plays. To Shakespeare in his lifetime John Davies of Hereford addressed some lines which most truly illustrate that nobility in his nature which stooped to no considerations of spite or revenge, such as were exhibited by other playwrights—*e.g.* Jonson, Dekker and Marston.

> 'Let others rail: but rail as they think fit,
> Thou hast no railing, but a reigning wit:
> And honesty thou sow'st, which they do reap.'

'Honesty': in other words 'the fine strains of honour.' Others may copy from him the tone of chivalry, of kings and courts, but Shakespeare is the king of courtesy. In him is instinct the 'reigning wit,' the 'wisdom' and 'royalty of nature' that were in Banquo.

In the matter of satire Shakespeare leaves us in no doubt as to the principles of his dramatic art. Theseus, splendidly impersonal and poetic, has the instinctive distaste of his creator for the drama which veils 'some satire, keen and critical.' There is only one poet whose character and quality are sketched for us in the Plays—the Poet of *Timon of Athens*. He is a base man who prostitutes his art for selfish, personal aims:

23

Does Shakespeare Rail?

'*Poet.* I am thinking what I shall say I have provided for him: it must be a personating of himself: a satire against the softness of prosperity, with a discovery of the infinite flatteries that follow youth and opulency.
Timon (aside). Must thou needs stand for a villain in thine own work? Wilt thou whip thine own faults in other men?'

Bad as the Poet is, he has a high conception of the business of Poetry. He fails in respect of personal motive, but there is art in the artist. Witness his speech to the Painter in the first scene:

'My free drift
Halts not particularly (*i.e.* is not arrested by personal considerations), but moves itself
In a wide sea of wax: no levell'd malice
Infects one comma in the course I hold:
But flies an eagle flight, bold and forth on,
Leaving no tract behind.'

Is it worth while further to demonstrate Shakespeare's abhorrence of satire and the judicial hypocrisy involved in anonymous censure of individuals? The Banished Duke may answer for him, when to Jaques, who claims for himself a charter as the wind, to blow on whom he pleases, he replies:

'Fie on thee! I can tell what thou wouldst do:
Most mischievous foul sin, in chiding sin:
For thou thyself hast been a libertine, etc.'*

* Jaques is a faint forecast of Timon: both have a passion for forests and caves. The remark of Apemantus might come with equal point from the mouth of the Banished Duke:
'Shame not these woods
By putting on the cunning of a carper.'

24

Does Shakespeare Rail?

Orlando, when invited by Jaques to join with him in railing against 'our mistress, the world,' makes not less emphatic answer: 'I will chide no breather in the world but myself, against whom I know most faults.'

'Leaving no tract behind.' Is it not rightly said of Shakespeare himself by the Poet whose aim he idealises? Idle is it to look in all that he wrote for an unkind speech against friend or enemy—if enemies he had—idle to look for any conscious reference to himself or confidences about the incidents of his life. It is not the way of the Elizabethan dramatist to inform posterity and puzzle his audience about his private concerns: it is not the way of any good Drama. In 154 Sonnets Shakespeare discourses, in every imaginable way, of friends and loves, and leaves himself and them an insoluble enigma. 'God's spy,' he looks out from the 'wall'd prison' of petty incident and mean surroundings on 'the mystery of things,' happy that, forgetting himself, he can 'pray and sing and tell old tales and laugh at gilded butterflies.' Amid the falsities of a conventional world he, like Hamlet, has an amused tolerance of Osric, while himself 'voyaging through strange seas of Thought, *alone.*' His stage children are very real to him: a phantom he seemed to himself, if all that he does *not* tell of himself tells us this. Lucy lies dead in Charlecote church—never for our purposes alive. Shallow lives, not in Cotswold Hills, where patient 'biography' digs for him, but in every place where

Does Shakespeare Rail?

garrulous senility and petty officialism have human form. The *genus* Shallow is everywhere: but Shakespeare's Shallow is individual, 'solely singular.' By what process was he evolved? Selection. It is a guess saying of Aubrey that 'Ben Johnson and he' (Shakespeare) 'did gather humours of men dayly, wherever they came.' It is a true saying, though Aubrey knew less of Shakespeare than he did of Jonson, and had most in mind those 'humours,' or character-types, on and with which Jonson worked. In his earlier comedies Shakespeare worked on the same materials and with the like tools. Gradually the figures took on themselves the thews of singularity, spoke with voices and moved with antics of their own. Sir Hugh Evans is a specialised Holofernes: Dogberry is a sublimated Dull. How his puppets became vitalised Shakespeare not obscurely tells. The process is conceived, if hardly yet confessed, in *Love's Labour's Lost* where Holofernes pre-figures its threefold stages—observation, rumination, adaptation. For himself he claims 'a foolish, extravagant spirit, full of forms, figures, objects, ideas, apprehensions, notions, revolutions: these are begot in the ventricle of memory, nourished in the womb of *pia mater*, and delivered on the mellowing of occasion.' Unworthy though he be, Jaques, like the Poet in *Timon*, speaks sometimes for Shakespeare, whose fashion in character-creation is of a piece with the 'melancholy' of Jaques, 'compounded of many simples, extracted from many objects, and indeed

William Shakespeare, Gentleman

the sundry observation of my travels, which by often rumination, wraps me in a most humorous sadness.' *Hic et ubique* is Shakespeare's method. Shallow is to be found in every county of England. As little need this or that shadowy master of Stratford school be dressed up for the part of Holofernes or Parson Evans. In Shakespeare's world there were Pantaloons and Pedants enough to stock a gallery of portraits without troubling Stratford for sitters.

§ 6 WILLIAM SHAKESPEARE, GENTLEMAN

Having considered the method of the dramatist, let us turn to the nature and breeding of the man, as set down in the recorded impressions of those who were his contemporaries and friends. Among them was John Davies of Hereford, whose lines on Shakespeare's 'reigning wit' I have already quoted: they are contained in a book by him called *The Scourge of Folly*, published about 1611, and are part of an eight-line epigram addressed to 'Our English Terence, Mr Will Shakespeare.' The lines preceding this quotation run:

'Some say (good Will), which I in sport do sing,
  Hadst thou not played some kingly parts in sport,
  Thou hadst been a companion for a King,
  And been a King among the meaner sort.'

That, surely, is a remarkable tribute of admiration. In the title of the epigram Davies addresses Will as a dramatist: but the lines convey the popular

27

William Shakespeare, Gentleman

impression of him as an actor. Players were not usually esteemed gentlemen in Shakespeare's day. But, says Davies, apart from his written plays there was something in the man, more than physical presence, more than adaptability to high scenic parts, that suggested a loftiness that would befit kings' chambers.

In 1603, when Shakespeare was not less famous as an actor than as a dramatist, the same writer says in a book entitled *Microcosmos*:

'Players, I love ye and your Quality,
As ye are men that pass time not abused:
And some I love for painting, poesy,
And say fell Fortune cannot be excused
That hath for better uses you refused:
Wit, courage, good shape, good parts, and all good,
As long as all these *goods* are no worse used:
And though the stage doth stain pure gentle blood,
Yet generous ye are in mind and mood.'

In the margin, against the third line, Davies put the initials R. B. W. S., which obviously stand for Richard Burbage and William Shakespeare. As 'painting' refers to Burbage, who had some reputation in that line, so 'poesy' refers to Shakespeare. Davies means that the two players had secondary gifts of genius, and that the twofold 'quality' of each of them fitted them for stations above the 'ungentle' profession of players. Nothing is in either of them that does not promise 'all good'— intelligence, confidence, good looks, good breeding. In a word, they are 'generous,' and in Elizabethan phrase 'generous' meant exactly what *generosus*

28

William Shakespeare, Gentleman

meant in descriptive style—'gentleman,' one who
has the essential marks which should distinguish
birth and breeding. One thinks of the woolman's
shop and that 'brute part' of calf-killing: and one
wonders.

The epithet 'sweet,' frequently applied to Shakespeare by contemporaries and the generation after
them, was a common one of poets and need have
no reference to character. But 'gentle' was more
peculiarly his own, and most of those who so described him were personal friends. The earliest
instance of its application is in Spenser's *Colin
Clout's come home again* (1595), where of 'Aëtion' it
is said:

'A gentler spirit may no where be found,
Whose Muse, full of high thought's invention,
Doth like himself heroically sound.'

I make no question that Aëtion is Shakespeare:
no other poet of the time had heroical invention
corresponding to a heroical surname.

Next come Ben Jonson's lines facing the Droes-
hout portrait in the First Folio:

'The figure that thou here seest put
It was for gentle Shakespeare cut.'

Again in Jonson's verses 'To the Memory of my
beloved the Author, Mr William Shakespeare,' he
addresses him as 'my gentle Shakespeare.'

In some cases the adjective is suggested by the
character of the writings rather than of the man.
Thus the players, in their 'Address to the Great

William Shakespeare, Gentleman

Variety of Readers,' say that he 'as he was a happy imitator of Nature, was a most gentle expresser of it.' And Jonson, in his *Timber* (1641), writes, 'He was indeed honest (*i.e.* honourable) and of an open, free nature: had an excellent Phantsie, brave notions and gentle expressions.' As Jonson was more apt to panegyrise the private qualities of the friend, whom he loved, than the dramatist, who in his judgment 'faulted,' we may take it from him that the 'gentleness' of Shakespeare was discovered as much in social intercourse as in anything that he wrote.

The tradition of his special amiability and sincerity seems to have survived 'among gentlemen of the neighbourhood' (Stratford) when Rowe wrote (1709), 'His exceeding candor and good nature must certainly have inclin'd all the gentler part of the world to love him.' The tradition was constant after his death. Suckling (before 1641) speaks of him as 'my friend, Mr William Shakespeare,' though he could have had no acquaintance with him, and styles him 'gentle Shakespeare,' contrasting him with 'the sweat of learned Jonson's brain.' Sir John Denham and James Howell (both in 1647) repeat the epithet and the contrast with Jonson. In 1658 Sir Aston Cokain writes of 'the gentle and ingenuous Shakespeare Muse': and in 1662 Margaret Cavendish in the General Prologue to her Plays repeats the adjective.

Whether 'gentle' relates to the books or to the man matters not at all in Shakespeare's case: for

William Shakespeare, Gentleman

of him it may be said more confidently than of any writer, before or since, that the style, 'the expression,' 'the invention' was the Man. Most truly is it said of him by Jonson:

> 'Look, how the father's face
> Lives in his issue, even so the race
> Of Shakespeare's mind and manners brightly
>   shines
> In his well turned and true-filed lines.'

'Candour,' 'free nature' is inseparable from the manner, but is not all. 'Gentleness,' as an Elizabethan understood the word, meant more than this —much more than it has come to mean in modern speech. Emphatically Shakespeare was a gentleman, and that not in the conventional sense in which he and fellow-dramatists wrote themselves 'gentleman' in the titles of their published plays. Gentle birth, supposed or real, might be an element in 'gentleness.' John Fletcher was a bishop's son and had the courtly tone: but nobody called him 'gentle.' Education had more to do with it than is conceived in modern ideas. Marlowe was a Cambridge graduate: Jonson was brought up at Westminster School under that prince of scholars, William Camden; nobody dreamt of calling either of them 'gentle.'

'Gentle,' in Shakespeare's phrase, is the constant style of kings and nobles when they are addressed by subjects or inferiors. 'Gentleness' is assumed in them, as mercifulness in the Almighty. 'Gentil herte is fulfild of pitee,' says Chaucer of King Alla.

William Shakespeare, Gentleman

Most nearly Shakespeare approached the divine in pity for the weak, the erring, the criminal, in comprehension of the soul of goodness in things evil, in the gracious kindliness of his dealing with women. With the courtly Laises of Fletcher contrast the pathetic figure of poor Doll Tearsheet, foul of speech, ingrained with dirt—and with a lingering womanly affection which makes her ending as tragical as Falstaff's—'O, the pity of it, Iago!' 'Nothing,' says Coleridge, 'ever left a stain on gentle Shakespeare's mind, which looked upon the degraded men and things around him, like moonshine on a dunghill, which shines and takes no pollution. All things are shadows to him, except those which move his affections.' In the 113th Sonnet he tells how his 'most true mind' makes his eye 'untrue' by turning the ugliest features of realism to a beauty born of sympathy and imagination:

'For if it (*i.e.* the eye) see the rud'st or gentlest sight,
The most sweet favour or deformed'st creature,
The mountain or the sea, the day or night,
The crow or dove, it shapes them'

to the image of what to him is most lovable.

Shakespeare, alone of his fellows in poetry, was 'all good,' had all the elements which are combined in 'gentleness':

'His life was gentle, and the elements
So mix'd in him that Nature might stand up,
And say to all the world "This was a man".'

What had Stratford to do with making of such a man?

32

Concerning Genius

§ 7 CONCERNING GENIUS

'But then,' cries Stratford, 'Genius! Genius defies conditions, oversteps ordinary law, works miracles.' 'Nothing almost sees miracles,' I would reply, but the obstinacy of Orthodoxy, which is the denial of Faith and Reason. Genius only works with supplied materials. The Stratfordian apologist* cites as exemplifying 'the mysterious origin and miraculous processes of all poetic genius' the cases of Chatterton, Burns, Keats, 'and other poets of humbler status and fortune than Shakespeare.' Who the 'other poets' may be I do not know. To thrust Chatterton into the company of Shakespeare is ridiculous. Burns is at home with cottars and ploughmen, very uncomfortable in Edinburgh drawing-rooms, and his stock of reading is of the smallest. The suggested parallel of Keats is most unfortunate. He was the son of a well-to-do father, and he had an excellent schooling which included Latin and French. His master was the father of his friend, Charles Cowden Clarke. He started life with books at hand and in the company of literary friends. In one respect his experience was not unlike the supposed experience of Shakespeare: for a short time he was an apprentice—but to a surgeon, not to a butcher.

A far better instance of untutored genius is that of Dickens, the circumstances of whose upbringing

---

* Sir Sidney Lee, *Life of Shakespeare* (1913), p. 655.

Concerning Genius

furnish an almost exact parallel to those of the
legendary Shakespeare. The unthrift father, the
huddling brothers and sisters*, the stunted education, the blacking-factory, the petty, sordid surroundings—are they not close counterparts of what
we are told to believe of Stratford Shakespeare's
lot? And the result? The genius of the novelist,
only comparable with that of the poet, is circum-
scribed by the conditions of early life. For books,
he knew as much, or as little, of the *Decline and Fall*
as, in the mouths of Dr Blimber or Mr Boffin, re-
semble Touchstone's citation of Ovid. In upper-
class society he is as awkward as Mr Guppy at
Chesney Wold or Mr Pickwick in the pump-room
at Bath. Of country sports he knows nothing. His
feet are glued to the pavement: the gloom of
Lincolnshire fills him with horror. Unreal children
wander in unreal fields and chatter with idyllic
schoolmasters and sextons (Evans and the Grave-
diggers!). The moral ugliness of 'society' is only
redeemed by simpletons who are outside it: 'the
glass of fashion, and the mould of form'—what
knows Dickens of Hamlet? Government and the
governing class are perverse and foolish: something
his reporting experiences told him of Taper and
Tadpole, nothing of Ulysses. Such was the actual
world of Dickens: Gonzalo's commonwealth never
entered his vision. Yet one advantage was given
to Dickens which was denied to the Stratford

* Oddly, John Dickens, like John Shakespeare, had a family
of seven children.

34

apprentice. He was introduced in early days to all the turmoil and variety of London streets. Mr Weller senior prided himself on the education which he allowed to his son of running in the streets, sleeping in markets, etc. That was a larger experience of life than was afforded by Henley Street.

The parallel between Dickens and the legendary William of Stratford may be carried further—if that can be called a parallel which ends in divergence. Genius, let us say again, is conditioned by environment. The youthful environment in either case being limited, it was natural and inevitable for either of them to recur, especially in their early work, to scenes familiar from boyhood. Dickens saturated himself in Rochester and the road to it travelled by the Pickwickians and David Copperfield. To it as 'Dulborough' and 'Cloisterham' his mind reverted, indeed, in later life: but that was after he had settled near it at Gadshill. Shakespeare's imagination was not tied to things seen, whether people or places, as Dickens was tied, but wherever he lays the scene of his earlier plays— whether it be Athens or Navarre—the real landscape is of Warwickshire. It is rural Warwickshire with scenes of forest glades and hunting parties, pictures of country clods and parsons and squires, with an occasional background of an abbey or monastic ruin. But 'Dulborough' does not come into the picture in any one of his plays, early or late, and his highway to London does not touch it, goes in fact far wide of it. Like Dickens, in later life he settled far from London amid the haunts of his youth: there at least he designed a family home. But it was not with him as it was with Dickens at Gadshill: in his later plays the local touch is wanting. Bohemia might be Warwickshire, but it might equally well be any pastoral shire in England. What may we surmise? That until he bade farewell to the theatre in the epilogue of the *Tempest*, he was only an occasional visitor to Stratford: such documented facts as remain to us point to residence in London before 1611.

§ 8 STRATFORD FACT AND FABLE

Of Stratford, where Shakespeare is supposed to have passed the first twenty-five years, or so, of his life, something it is unavoidable to say. So much has already been written about it that I shall, as far as possible, avoid repetition.

It was a place of minor consequence, even in Warwickshire. It had no history. As a centre of trade and population it did not compare with Coventry. It had no lordly castle such as that which dignified Warwick. There had never been any important monastic house in or near the town. No magnate or county gentleman had his residence there. No inhabitant had ever distinguished himself in letters or in national affairs. *Vervecum patria*: it was a pelting place whose wisest talk was of fells and tods of wool and the price of ewes.

Stratford Fact and Fable

It had a school, which was much as other schools in the county, but not as Coventry, where Philemon Holland once taught and where George, Lord Berkeley and probably Marston, the dramatist, were once pupils. How little the leading inhabitants profited by its existence is shown by the fact that of nineteen persons (ten of them aldermen) who signed a paper relating to one of their body, seven only could write their names. John Shakespeare, William's father, was one of the illiterate majority. In the Legend a good deal is made of the maternal influence on the young poet. Mary Arden, daughter of a farmer and small land-owner, was scarcely more likely than Audrey to have poetical tastes: she, too, made her mark. An attempt has been made to alleviate the illiteracy of John. Diligent research has unearthed the fact that once he had a book in his keeping: what it was, how he came by it, whether he could and did read it, nobody can depone.* At Warwick and at Kenilworth the Dudleys had books, and at a rather later time Philemon Holland gathered a notable library at Coventry, to which Lucius Cary, the famous Lord Falkland, often resorted in his schooldays. At Stratford nobody had any use for books, and nobody traded in them. Be it admitted that, long after Shakespeare's schooldays and at a time when education had made much advance, there died, in 1609, a curate of Bishopton, Stratford, named John Marshall, who was possessor of something more

* Mrs Stopes, *Shakespeare's Environment*, p. 61.

37

than a hundred books. Three-fourths of them were theological: the rest were mostly such ordinary classical books as a University man might be expected to have. There were a few English books, of which Ascham's *Scholemaster* was the only one of any literary value.

It is assumed, not without probability, by the Traditionalists, that young Shakespeare was entered at the Town Free School, and, more doubtfully, that his age at admission was seven. It is conceded by them that his father's embarrassments, beginning in the year 1577, led to his withdrawal at the age of thirteen. At such an age it might be presumed that he had got beyond the elements of Latin and, being of precocious 'wit,' had compassed some Ovid and Terence, possibly some extracts from Virgil and Sallust, etc. English, of course, had no part in the school curriculum. After his schooldays it is in the last degree unlikely that the supposed apprentice increased his scanty stock of book knowledge, unless we invent a Stratford somebody who was interested in the youth's education and competent to further it and arouse his interest. If such a person existed, his friendly 'coaching' must have altogether ceased when Shakespeare married at the age of eighteen. The penniless apprentice could have had no books of his own, and where or of whom could he acquire books at Stratford? Autolycus, no doubt, brought a fardel of ballads to sell at fair-times: his pack would hardly include a folio of Chaucer or even such a popular collection as Tottel's *Miscellany*.

Into the thorns of the question of Shakespeare's learning I do not venture. I am content to accept Jonson's verdict of 'less Greek,' and am not disposed to deny that, judged by the Jonsonian standard, his Latin was 'small.' This does not exclude the likelihood that Beeston was right in saying that he understood Latin 'pretty well,' and I am quite sure that, however small it might be, the ventricle of his memory was extraordinarily retentive of it. The fruit that he had noted in spring blossoming and watched in dreaming summer he gathered for use on the mellowing of occasion. Jonson's berries are crude and harsh, lacking the seasoning of opportunity. Shakespeare's use for Latin is to change it to English. The scene of *Venus* is not Ovidian but English, and Venus herself is a more outspoken Phoebe. It is much the same with his vocabulary, wherein his fertility far surpasses Jonson's, and the more part of his fire-new words comes from Latin sources: if their meaning is in doubt it is a good plan to consult Cooper's *Thesaurus* (1565).

Classical Latin was but a part of Shakespeare's store. It is scarcely possible to fix the time at which he made acquaintance with the work of his predecessors in English poetry, Surrey, Sackville, Sidney and Spenser, from whom he learnt the cadences of his verse. From Chaucer he derived the seven-line stanza of *Lucrece*, and the six-line stanza of *Venus* was perhaps suggested by Spenser's *Astrophel* (1586). Where and when did he get the chance of handling English books? Certainly not at Stratford. Perhaps in London in those uncertain years which he spent there before the publication of *Venus*. To allow plenty of time for making acquaintance with them the Traditional date assigned to his Hegira is about 1585, the year in which his twins were born. It is a pure guess. Whatever the date might be, I cannot think that his first introduction to English books was after he came to London, when the hypothesis would make him to be twenty-one years old. The appetite and the interest must surely have begun at an earlier, more receptive and more leisurely time.

§ 9 THE FLIGHT TO LONDON

The Charlecote legend being dismissed, one has to ask—Why did Shakespeare leave Stratford? Of course he made a fool of himself when he married Anne (or Agnes), who, it may be supposed, was incapable of understanding his genius and not unreasonably querulous to a husband who, having introduced her to penury, spent in penning stanzas the time which should be given to the wool business, supposing the Stratford story to be true. 'The dark house and the detested wife' and the second-best bed, all surmise being permissible, may pass as a clue to his motive. But I confess to a sentimental feeling that such treachery was not what I should

The Flight to London

expect of 'my gentle Shakespeare'—a treachery to children as well as wife, and particularly to unhappy, bankrupt John. Conceive the situation. William and Anne with three babes are living in a small house, the unwelcome guests and pensioners of John and Mary, who have five children of their own: and the shutters are up in the woolshop, and there is no wage or occupation for the apprentice. The notion that he joined a travelling company of actors may be dismissed: of all trades the player's is one of the most precarious, and no touring company was likely to encumber itself with an untrained youth. As Sir Sidney Lee remarks, 'When a company of city actors took the road, it reduced its personnel to a minimum: and even so, the large London companies barely made their expenses on tour.' And even if the story told by the Stratford parish clerk in 1693, that Shakespeare 'was received into the playhouse as a serviture,' had any likelihood, it is inconceivable that the chance of getting such a job would draw him to London. Some more definite prospect he must have had, and there is no ground for supposing that, about 1585, his thoughts turned to a profession which afforded such small encouragement to an untried youth who was father of a family.

If Shakespeare had made an unwise marriage, he was nevertheless, as all records show, shrewd enough in all practical matters. In his pocket he had a key, which happened to be a key of gold. 'What a fool, quoth he, am I to lie in a stinking

The Flight to London

Dungeon, when I may as well walk at liberty. I
have a Key in my bosom, called Promise, that will,
I am persuaded, open any lock in Doubting Castle.'
Was it the Promise of the Stage? I think not.

'While Johnson kept his academy, there can be
no doubt that he was insensibly furnishing his
mind with various knowledge: but I have not discovered that he wrote anything except a great part
of his tragedy of IRENE....Mr Walmsley was well
pleased with this proof of Johnson's abilities as a
dramatick writer, and advised him to finish the
tragedy and produce it on the stage....Johnson
now thought of trying his fortune in London, the
great field of genius and exertion, where talents of
every kind have the fullest scope and the highest
encouragement.'

Supposing that Beeston was right about 'the
schoolmaster in the country,' does not Boswell's
account fit the case of Shakespeare singularly well?
Boswell goes on to say that Johnson found little
encouragement from the gentleman in London to
whom he had been recommended. Shakespeare
had surer prospects, for he took with him a letter
of introduction to the Earl of Southampton. At
least that is the probability which I hope to set up.

§ 10 SHAKESPEARE'S SILENCE ABOUT
STRATFORD

We may take it as unquestionable fact that William
was born at Stratford in 1564, and had children
born to him there in 1583 and 1585. Between 1564
and the date of his acquisition of New Place in 1597

42

Shakespeare's Silence about Stratford

there is no recorded fact which establishes his continuous abode there. It is of course likely enough that some part of the years between 1571 and 1577 is to be filled up with attendance at the Free School. The gossip of people who lived two or three generations after the poet's death and knew nothing of him in the years of his retirement interposes some foolish and contradictory tales of his apprenticeship, which presumably lasted for the seven years from 1577 to 1584, and therefore should have overlapped his marriage year*. If he lived at Stratford for twenty-one years at least, there should be a likelihood that in his writings, so full of Warwickshire scenes in his early plays, there would be some incidental allusions to a place with which he had so many associations. There are none to Stratford, next to none to any place near it. Only by constrained exegesis can any passage be tortured into an allusion to Stratford which might not equally well be referred to any other place.

There is, of course, a reference to the Lucy arms, visible at Charlecote, out of which so much fable has been compiled. There is mention of a place called Wincote or Woncote, which has been supposed to be the hamlet called Wilmecote or Wincote, a few miles from Stratford: of that I shall speak presently. And there is the fact that Shakespeare

* 'To enter a craft a youth served an apprenticeship of seven years, living for this period in his master's house as one of the family, being, as a rule, fed and clothed and taught by him and given an increasing amount of pocket-money.' *Minutes and Accounts of Stratford on Avon Corporation* (1921), vol. I, p. xlii.

Shakespeare's Silence about Stratford

locates Justice Shallow in the neighbourhood of the Cotswold Hills, the near end of which is some twelve miles southward from Stratford: of that, too, something remains to be said. In any case to know Cotswold and the coursing games alluded to in *Merry Wives* needed no residence at Stratford or the neighbourhood: they were almost as famous as Goodwood is to-day, and it is to be noted that the fallow greyhound that was 'outrun on Cotsall' belonged, not to Shallow or Slender of Gloucestershire, but to Page of Windsor. The games were celebrated in verse in a volume entitled *Annalia Dubrensia* (1636)—from the name of their promoter, Robert Dover—by poets so foreign to the locality as Jonson and Drayton, and the woodcut which serves as frontispiece to the book gives prominence to coursing. Gloucestershire dogs were famous: Edward Alleyne procured them for baiting at Paris Gardens*. The only place in South Warwickshire of which Shakespeare makes direct and certain mention is Barton-on-the-Heath, where Christopher Sly's father lived. It is a village some twenty miles distant from Stratford and close to the Oxfordshire border. Its name was suggested to Shakespeare by the circumstance that his maternal aunt, Joan Lambert, and her husband lived there†.

* Warner, *Catalogue of MSS. at Dulwich College*, pp. 71, 72.
† Sir Sidney Lee's craving to discover any reference to Stratford in the Plays leads him to remark, 'There was a genuine Stephen' (not Christopher) 'Sly, who was in the dramatist's day a self-asserting citizen of Stratford.' As the Drunkard is called Slie in the old *Taming of a Shrew*, which was not written

44

Shakespeare's Silence about Stratford

Sir Sidney Lee—for no stated reason—says that 'the poaching episode is best assigned to the year 1585*.' He continues,

'It was doubtless in the early summer of 1586 that Shakespeare first traversed the road to the capital....His first journey to London may well have been made on foot. There were two main routes by which London was approached from Stratford, one passing through Oxford and High Wycombe, and the other through Banbury and Aylesbury....Tradition points to the Oxford and High Wycombe road as Shakespeare's favoured thoroughfare.'

It has been so generally assumed that one or other of these routes was taken by Shakespeare in his travels to London, that Dr Furnivall in his reprint of Harrison's *Description of England* (New Shakespeare Society, 1881) inserted in it a reduction of the Ordnance Map in which the two roads are marked in colour. It is likely enough that, when Shakespeare had settled himself at Stratford and given up writing plays, he followed one or other of them. But it is odd that in his plays he indicates

by Shakespeare, the notion that Shakespeare had in mind a Stratford acquaintance is purely illusory.

* A Mr Dowdall, visiting Stratford in 1693, was informed by the parish clerk, who gave himself out to be over eighty years old, though he was actually only sixty-five, that Shakespeare was formerly apprenticed to a butcher there (apparently not his father), but that 'he ran from his master to London.' If he was an apprentice at the time of his flight to London, that event could scarcely be later than 1584. But no credence is to be given to such foolishness. An Oxford graduate, who visited Stratford a year later than Dowdall, sensibly remarks that clerks and sextons 'are for the most part a very ignorant sort of people.'

Shakespeare's Silence about Stratford

no familiarity with any place that lies on them. Of the five stopping-places which Sir Sidney Lee mentions (*Life*, p. 40 *note*), he does not mention one. He does very clearly indicate another road from Warwickshire to London, but that road takes him far away from Stratford. Oxford is only known to him as the place where Silence had a son at the University, and Banbury merely suggests to Bardolph the opprobrious similitude, 'Banbury cheese,' applied to Slender. Sir Sidney Lee cites 'tradition' in support of his allegation: and in the absence of Gospel, Tradition is a very present help. First, there is Aubrey's rash statement that at Grendon, Bucks—'near Oxford,' Sir Sidney interpolates, though it is a long way from Oxford, not in Oxfordshire, and not on the Oxford-London main road— Shakespeare 'happened to take the humour of the constable in *Midsummer Night's Dream*,' and Aubrey adds, 'I think it was Midsummer Night that he happened to lie there.' Absurd and blundering as Aubrey's story is, it is enough for present purposes to say that Shakespeare bought New Place at Stratford in 1597, two or three years before the production of *Much Ado*. Then, says Sir Sidney, 'the Crown Inn, at Oxford, was long pointed out as one of the dramatist's favourite resting-places.' Of course he is alluding to the incredible scandal of Shakespeare's *liaison* with Mrs Davenant, wife of the innkeeper of the Crown. As Sir William Davenant, the shameless author of this and other mendacities about Shakespeare, was born in 1605–6,

Shakespeare's Silence about Stratford

the silly story is no evidence for the period preceding the purchase of New Place*.

There is yet stronger evidence that, when he wrote the First Part of *Henry IV*, Shakespeare was unfamiliar with the Stratford-London road and uninterested in Stratford itself. In that play there is battle brewing near Shrewsbury, and the King and Prince Hal from London are making what haste they can to get there. By what route should they go? If a straight line be drawn from London to Shrewsbury it passes exactly through Stratford, and the direct line is continued thence through Bridgenorth. That is the route which Shakespeare, who does not take his authority from Holinshed, makes the King to follow, while the Prince makes a detour south of Stratford.

> 'Our meeting
> Is Bridgenorth: and, Harry, you shall march
> Through Gloucestershire: by which account,
> Our business valued, some twelve days hence
> Our general forces at Bridgenorth shall meet.'

Does Falstaff take the direct way by Stratford, or does he take the less direct through Gloucestershire? Neither. He makes a wide detour through northern Warwickshire, and is at some pains to tell us what places lay about his march from London.

* Sir Sidney Lee's statement that Shakespeare stood godfather to Davenant in 1605—Davenant was born in 1605–6—has no better foundation than a miserable old 'chestnut' told by Hearne in 1709, and by him fastened on Shakespeare. The story as told by John Taylor in 1630 had nothing in it about Shakespeare, Davenant or Oxford.

47

Shakespeare's Silence about Stratford

Something lies behind this mystery. If only Shakespeare had willed that Falstaff's ragged prodigals should take the Stratford road, what a chance he had for local scenes and characters!—obsequious justices entertaining Falstaff in their parlour, Bardolph's fiery face filling the lattice in the Bear Inn, Shallow with Silence in the Rother Market discussing the price of ewes and bullocks and the certainty of death. And Shakespeare, who to a London audience presented that 'jest unseen, inscrutable' about Lucy of Charlecote, missed the obvious opportunity, and that poor place, Sutton Coldfield, not native Stratford, had the glory of beholding Falstaff in the flesh. Or supposing that Falstaff had chosen to march with Prince Hal through Gloucestershire, was not that the occasion for making acquaintance with Shallow? But Shallow's entrance is delayed until the Second Part and a time when Falstaff had no obvious reason for going to Gloucestershire.

§ 11 CONCERNING ARDEN

Here is another matter not unworthy of consideration. Granted that Lodge laid the scene of his *Rosalynde* in the Arden of France, I cannot doubt that in his play Shakespeare had in mind the Warwickshire Arden, which also supplied him with the woodland scenery of *Midsummer Night's Dream*. When Milton wrote of Shakespeare's 'native wood-notes' he was thinking of the comedies which gave

PLATE I

THE GATEHOUSE OF POLESWORTH ABBEY

FROM THE STREET

him the setting of *Comus*, and probably he thought that native Stratford was in the woodland. In strictness this was not so. The county of Warwick, Camden tells us, consisted of two districts, the Feldon, 'a champaign country' of cornfields and pastures, and the Woodland, otherwise called Arden. The Feldon was in the southern part and was divided from the Woodland by the Avon. Stratford was therefore on the edge of the forest, but not actually in it: Camden reckons it as in the Feldon. But there is a group of villages which have, or had, the distinguishing addition to their names 'in Arden.' They are all in the central or more northerly parts of Warwickshire or in the neighbouring county of Leicester—Drayton, Hampton, Overton (otherwise Orton-on-the-Hill), Polesworth, Tanworth, Weston. Henley in Arden is nearest to Stratford, eight miles distant. Ardens Grafton, some six miles west of Stratford, as Dugdale tells us, took its name, not from the forest, but from the Warwickshire family of Arden.

It is a thing to be remarked that, putting aside *As You Like It*, Shakespeare's earlier comedies, *Love's Labour's Lost*, *The Two Gentlemen of Verona* and *Midsummer Night's Dream* are all, more or less, associated with woodland scenes. It will be said that, though Stratford is not actually in Arden, it was sufficiently near it to account for Shakespeare's familiarity with forest landscape. But the scene of *Love's Labour's Lost* is very definitely in a country parish, lacking any suggestion of a neighbouring

town. The title of the Quarto of 1598 says that
the play was 'presented before her Highness this
last Christmas,' and that in its form as then printed
it was 'newly corrected and augmented.' Though
no printed edition of earlier date is known to exist,
the text of the First Folio is so discrepant from that
of the Quarto that it is clear that an earlier draft
of the play was consulted by Heminge and Condell.
It is at least not improbable that in its original
form the play was intended for a performance
before the Queen on the occasion of her visit, in
August 1591, to Titchfield, Southampton's home,
and Cowdray, where it is on record that she killed
'prickets' in the park of Lord Montagu, Southampton's uncle. The play has all the marks of a
first exercise in comedy. It has no progress or
plot, resembling therein any one of Gilbert's
extravaganzas, gyrating playfully about a postu-
lated absurdity. In structural skill it is as inferior
to the *Two Gentlemen* as it surpasses it in poetical
fancy. It was not Shakespeare's way to stage the
actual men and women whom he knew. Holofernes
is not John Florio, and Moth is certainly not
Thomas Nash. But in *Love's Labour's Lost* he does
give a picture of the society in which he moved in
his early days, and the picture is not that of
Stratford. The King, the Princess and their com-
panions are just such people as might be found about
the country house of a refined Elizabethan gentleman. Sir Nathaniel is described as a 'hedge-priest,'
not unlike Sir Oliver Martext, 'vicar of the next

village' to Arden. Holofernes is a country pedagogue, who organises a rustic 'shew,' just as the
schoolmaster, Gerrold, does in the *Two Noble
Kinsmen**. He keeps a school at 'the charge-house,'
whatever that might be, on the top of a hill, and
he educates girls as well as boys, as was never the
case in town schools. Dull is a village 'thar-
borough,' such as Marian Hacket of Wincote went
to seek. Costard, like any rustic misdemeanant, is
not sent to gaol, but committed to the custody of
a local squire. Deer-park and lodge betray the
lord of the demesne—Shallow, it may be, who had
both, but not Charlecote Lucy who had no deer-
park. Cuckoo and Owl, daisies pied and bleaching
smocks make up a picture without the background
of Stratford town.

In Speed's map (1610) the whole of Warwickshire, north of the Avon, is shown covered with
trees. Camden (1586) describes this region as 'for
the most part cloathed with woods, yet it wants
not pastures nor cornfields, and it hath also several
veins of iron.' In the eighteenth century Gough
adds, 'The ironworks in the counties round destroyed such prodigious quantities of wood that
they laid the country more open, and by degrees
made room for the plough.' In the pretty tenth
Nimphall of his *Muses Elizium* (1630) Drayton
deplores the displacement of 'Silvanus and his

---

* Holofernes and Gerrold are fellows in pedantry. Their
prototype is Schoolmaster Rombus in Sidney's masque of
The Mayladie presented to Queen Elizabeth at Wanstead.

woody crue' and the 'jocund life' of Felicia (*i.e.* Arden) by 'the beastly men that all those great and goodly Woods destroy'd':

'The lofty hie Wood, and the lower spring
Sheltering the Deare in many a suddaine showre,
Where Quires of Birds oft wonted were to sing,
The flaming Furnace wholly doth devoure.'

Though this destruction had begun in Shakespeare's day, the country generally preserved its wooded appearance. Robert Herrick has a pleasant description of it in a letter, dated 1612, addressed to his brother, Emanuel:

'Touching our progres and our business in the frontyers of Warwick and Staffordshire, I would you had been with us, you would have thought it a pleasant journey. . .where you know that suche youthes as I am do more delight in the pleasant woods of Kanke*, and to hear the sweet birds sing, the hammers goe, and betells in the paper mylles at the same place also. . .and now find as good iron as was there this 40 year, as good wayght, as good workmen, as onest fellows, as good intertainment. What would you have more? As for pakkenedells, hawkes bells, leurs and the rest I will make no answer.'

As there is so much talk of deer in *As You Like It*, it is worth remarking that Camden mentions several 'chaces' in Arden. There were also enclosed deer-parks. One of them was 'impaled' at Pooley, in Polesworth parish, by Sir Thomas Cokain in the

---

* Kank Wood, otherwise Cannock Chase, near Lichfield.

reign of Henry VIII*. Pasture, displacing trees, had already brought sheep and sheepcotes, and therewith the absentee masters 'of churlish disposition' whom Corin and his fellows of the forest had best reason to detest. Harrison, in his *Description of England*, remarks concerning the conversion of forest chases into enclosed parks and warrens that the former, though far greater in circuit, were less 'devourers of people,' inasmuch as they contained 'much tillage and many towns,' whereas parks had only a keeper's lodge, or at most a manor-house—whence Benedick's comparison, 'as melancholy as a lodge in a warren.'

§ 12 OF POETS, PATRONS AND PAGES

Let us concede to Tradition all, and more than all, that it asks for. Let us assume that Stratford school provided an education as good as the best that was given in any provincial school, and that Shakespeare profited by a schooling extending over some ten years and ending, not at thirteen, but at the less usual age of sixteen. Let us assume that the stories of his apprenticeship to a trade are idle talk: that his parents had 'eaten paper' and 'drunk ink,' contrary to all evidence: that a high degree of culture prevailed in the society of the little town. Let us grant all this: and then let us ask what is the likelihood that in the latter half of the sixteenth

* Speed's map shows twenty enclosed parks in the Woodland: only two in the Feldon, and none at Charlecote.

Of Poets, Patrons and Pages

century a provincial youth, son of a penniless father, educated solely at a country school, and lacking assistance from friends or patrons, would, at the age of twenty-nine, leap into the foremost place among poets of a time of first-class poetry, and emerge under the distinguished patronage of one of the greatest peers in England.

I take from the Index to Professor Saintsbury's *Elizabethan Literature* the names of all authors bred in England and born in the half-century 1550–1599, sixty-eight in all. They are of all classes in life and of all branches of authorship: some of them are very minor lights. According to the *Dictionary of National Biography* the places of education of ten of them (eleven if Shakespeare be included) are unrecorded*. Of the remaining fifty-eight no fewer than fifty-four were bred at the Universities or Inns of Court, and one, John Davies of Hereford, though not admitted at the University, lived at Oxford as a writing master. Two (Kyd and Jonson), who apparently did not proceed to a University, were taught at London schools (Merchant Taylors' and Westminster). One (Sylvester) was educated solely at a provincial school. If Shakespeare had no other education than what was given him at Stratford school, he must be placed in the same lowly class

* Of the unknown, Webster (? Merchant Taylors' School) and probably Dekker were Londoners: Field was one of the Children of the Queen's Chapel: Gervase Markham was brother of a knight: Izaak Walton was a London apprentice. Nothing is known of the education of Chapman, the two Rowleys and Tourneur. Of Drayton something will be said presently.

PLATE II

THE GATEHOUSE, POLESWORTH ABBEY   FROM THE INTERIOR

Of Poets, Patrons and Pages

as Joshuah Sylvester. But Sylvester was brought up at Southampton by the celebrated divine and schoolmaster, Hadrian à Saravia, who insisted that his boys should learn to converse in French, a circumstance which helped Sylvester in versifying the *Works and Days* of Du Bartas*.

We have seen a picture of William, husband and father, trudging to London, without friends there and without reasonable hope of getting a livelihood

* Nash, in his *Anatomie of Absurditie* (1590), is witness for the low estimation in which a provincial education was held as a qualification for the pursuit of poetry. Of the writers of 'new-found songs and sonnets which every red-nose fiddler hath at his fingers' end' he says, 'They contemn arts as unprofitable, contenting themselves with a little country-grammar knowledge.' In 1590 there could be no allusion to Shakespeare's Sonnets. Mr A. F. Leach, in his otherwise valuable account of Warwickshire schools (*Victoria History of Warwickshire*), remarks concerning masters at Stratford: 'Whatever the deficiencies of Hunt or Jenkins may have been, they were at all events sufficient scholars to give Shakespeare, the son of a Stratford glover and butcher, as good an education as Ben Jonson, the mason or bricklayer, received at Westminster.' Surely Mr Leach has gone much astray from the facts. Jonson was the son of a clergyman, though it is true that his mother took as her second husband a master builder. Has Mr Leach forgotten that Jonson's master at Westminster was William Camden of the *Britannia*, Clarencieux king-of-arms, the friend of all the scholars of his age? Has he forgotten that to that 'most learned and honoured friend' Jonson dedicated his *Every Man in his Humour*, and that in an epigram addressed to him he writes:
'Camden, most reverend head, to whom I owe
    All that I am in arts, all that I know'?
In the half-century, 1550–1599, Westminster and Merchant Taylors' were foremost among English schools. Famous among Westminster boys were Hakluyt, Bishop Henry King and probably Herrick. At Merchant Taylors', of which the celebrated Mulcaster was headmaster, Thomas Lodge, Spenser, Bishop Lancelot Andrewes and Shirley, the dramatist, were educated.

55

Of Poets, Patrons and Pages

there by his experience as butcher, glover, school-master, or whatever occupation Tradition assigns to him. It is a piece of pure guess-work and highly improbable as guess. It would be pleasant to hazard a likelier guess—that Shakespeare was one of the large class of 'University wits' to which most of his contemporaries in Poetry and Drama belonged. Things more impossible could be imagined, and, owing to the imperfection of University records of the time, no safe argument is to be based on the omission in them of his name. If he was entered at either University, his stay there must have been short and must have ended with his marriage at the age of eighteen. The writer of the Cambridge play, *The Return from Parnassus*, makes it plain that, if indeed he was ever at that University, the memory of his residence was lost in 1601–2. Kempe, the actor, says, 'Few of the Universitie pen plaies well, they smell too much of that writer, *Ovid*, and that writer, *Metamorphosis*. . . . Why here's our fellow, *Shakespeare*, puts them all down, aye, and *Ben Jonson* too.' But some definite prospect must have drawn Shakespeare to London. So far as we know, Stratford had given him no opportunity of proving himself in the quality of actor. His only merchandise and tools of trade were Poetry, and Poetry, without Patronage, was not a commodity to give lodging and livelihood in London.

Some introduction to London and some support when he got there I not doubtfully conclude that Shakespeare had. It could only come from a

Of Poets, Patrons and Pages

Warwickshire patron, and the patron must have had sufficient knowledge of the abilities and promise of his protégé to encourage the venture and to open his purse-strings.

Patronage in Shakespeare's day, and before and after it, was the almost invariable prop of needy authorship. In the sixteenth and seventeenth centuries it opened wide the doors of Education and Society to sons of provincial parsons, tradesmen and farmers, who otherwise were turned into the world to starve on such elements of learning as were given in local schools. Often the patron's interest carried the boy on to a University, or in other ways advanced him in his career. It was the huge advantage of these rural lads that they were rescued from the shop or the plough at an age when education was to begin and impressions were liveliest. Drayton tells us that he was

> 'a proper, goodly page,
> Much like a pygmy, scarce ten years of age,'

and that, at that age, he had a 'mild tutor,' who read to him 'honest Mantuan,' the author so much beloved by Holofernes, and afterwards Virgil's *Eclogues*.

Among authors who in boyhood were pages in the service of wealthy patrons the following may be mentioned: Chaucer, son of a London vintner, page to the Lady Elizabeth de Burgh, widow of Lionel, Duke of Clarence; John Hardyng, chronicler, page to Henry Percy ('Hotspur'); Sir Thomas More, placed at the age of thirteen in the household of

Of Poets, Patrons and Pages

Archbishop Morton; Sir Thomas Cokain, page to the Earl of Shrewsbury; Thomas Churchyard, page to the famous Earl of Surrey; William Davenant, son of an Oxford innkeeper, page to the Duchess of Richmond; Samuel Butler, son of a farmer, page to the Countess of Kent*.

In homes such as these the page found books, and had teachers such as the grammar-school boy had not. In his education, as Shakespeare ofttimes reminds us, singing was a principal part: and music and sweet poetry were in better agreement then than now†. And in such houses hung

* In Massinger's *Unnatural Combat*, iii, 2, the Page, 'a little wit in decimo sexto,' says, 'Ere I was sworn to the pantofle, I have heard my tutor' etc., from which it may be gathered that in some cases boys were tutored before they were taken into the service of ladies. In his Introductory Notice to the Plays of Massinger, Lt.-Col. Cunningham writes: 'In the dedication to his *A New Way to Pay Old Debts* the poet states that he was "born a devoted servant to the thrice noble family of Herbert," and the probability is that he was brought up as a page to the Countess of Pembroke at Wilton. His allusions to the situation and minor duties of pages are perpetual. In that particular place he would learn to admire the combination of rank and power and stately, yet flowing courtesy which in after-life he was so fond of bestowing upon his favourite characters. So successful is he in these delineations that, without the knowledge that such in all likelihood had been his upbringing, a biographer would be led to assume that it was so, in order to account for the confident and consummate ease with which he treads the halls, and ascends the staircases, and enters the tents, and sits down at the banquets of his great dukes and emperors and vice-roys and proconsuls.' *Mutato nomine* this applies equally to Shakespeare. It may account for his aristocratic sympathies and the lofty good-humour of his bearing to his humbler characters.

† Has any contemporary dramatist so many singing pages and gentlemen's 'boys' as Shakespeare? (*Love's Labour's Lost, Measure for Measure, As You Like It, Julius Caesar*). Who was his music master at Stratford?

Of Poets, Patrons and Pages

many 'a piece of skilful painting' such as that which is so elaborately described in *Lucrece*, or those other pictures of classical subjects which were offered for the delectation of Christopher Sly. Better than all, he was introduced to the refined society of cultivated gentlemen and, more especially, of ladies. In the Induction of the *Taming of the Shrew* the Lord, giving instructions how his page, Bartholo-mew, is to bear himself in the character of a noble lady, says:

'Tell him from me
He bear himself with honourable action,
Such as he hath observed in noble ladies
Unto their lords*.'

Conversely, ladies might readily assume the page's part: Julia, Jessica, Rosalind, Viola (the Duke's 'boy') and Imogen all do so. To the sharp wits of pages and the liberty of speech accorded to them the early plays bear ample testimony. The tutor was perhaps usually chaplain in the patron's household. In his perhaps earliest play, the Third Part of *Henry VI*, Shakespeare has a seeming re-miniscence of the kindly relations existing between such a tutor and his pupil. The scene is the battle of Wakefield. Enter Rutland and his Tutor: to whom young Rutland presently

'Ah, tutor, look where bloody Clifford comes.'

To them enter Clifford and his soldiers: *loquitur* Clifford:

'Chaplain, away! thy priesthood saves thy life';

* Respecting pages and pageants, see pp. 117–118.

59

and he orders Rutland to be dragged off: then the Tutor:

> 'And I, my lord, will bear him company.
> *Clifford.* Soldiers, away with him!'
> [*Tutor is dragged off by Soldiers.*]*

§ 13 WHAT HAPPENED IN 1572

Where in Warwickshire should a patron be found to charge himself with the board and upbringing of young William? There were the princely establishments at the Castles of Warwick and Kenilworth, both in Shakespeare's youth in the possession of Robert Dudley, Earl of Leicester: and Dudley, in his cold, magnificent way, may be accounted a fosterer of learning and literary men. But his interests were centred in the Court, and it was at London that the 'Leicester set' gathered. There is no reason to suppose that John of Stratford had any such acquaintance with the Earl as to procure the admission of his son to either of his Warwickshire households. Moreover, about these great, historic sites Shakespeare is curiously silent. Warwick is mentioned only once, and that incidentally, in the Third Part of *Henry VI* (v, 1. 3): Kenilworth (Killingworth) occurs only once, in a probably un-Shakespearean scene of the Second Part (iv, 4. 39, 44). Yet Shakespeare probably passed both places in travelling between Stratford and Coventry.

---

* The incident is from the Chronicle of Hall, who describes him as 'chappelaine and scholemaster.'

What Happened in 1572

The idea that he was taken by his father to the Kenilworth pageants in 1575 is purely fanciful: if there be any allusion to them in *Midsummer Night's Dream* it was derived from the description of them in a pamphlet of 1576.

John Shakespeare held the office of High Bailiff, corresponding to that of Mayor, in 1568-9, and in September 1571 he was elected Chief Alderman. In the latter year the Legend supposes that William began his lessons at the Grammar School. John's financial embarrassments had scarcely begun—at least were not matter of notoriety. But his family was multiplying: in 1571 he had three children, besides William. A son who could so astonish his father by his proficiency in the Absey book possibly seemed to demand an education superior to that of the Grammar School. More likely John was simply concerned with the keep of an un-wage-earning boy.

It so happened that, just at this time, a matter was in dispute between the Corporation of Stratford and a townsman named Perret, and it was submitted to the arbitration of four county gentlemen— Sir Fulke Greville, Sir Thomas Lucy, Clement Throckmorton, and Henry Goodere of Polesworth. The arbitrators gave their award at Stratford on January 3, 1570-1, and were entertained by the Corporation at the Bear Inn in Bridge Street*. As John Shakespeare was a regular attendant in this

* The award is printed in *Minutes and Accounts of the Corporation of Stratford-upon-Avon*, 1533-1620, vol. ii, pp. 40-42. For drawing my attention to it I must thank Mr Bernard H. Newdigate of Stratford-on-Avon.

61

year at Corporation meetings—indeed was present at a meeting on January 18—it is all but certain that he made the acquaintance of Goodere in that month, if indeed it had not begun earlier. Twice in the accounts of 1571–2 the Corporation paid for horse-hire to 'Mr Gooderes,' and on January 18 in the same year it was agreed 'by the assent and consent of the aldermen and burgesses that Mr Adrian Queney, now baylif, and Mr John Shakespere shall at Hillary terme next ensuinge deale in the affayres concerninge the commen wealthe of the burroughe accordinge to theire discrecions.' The order apparently relates to litigation in London, but it is clear that in all its legal business the Corporation reposed its confidence in its Chief Alderman. What talk may have passed between him and Goodere it is impossible to say. But I take it that, then or later*, little William was packed off to Polesworth—a curious piece of good luck for him and for us: for in all England, outside London, there was then, and was to be later, no place more feracious of poetic genius than Polesworth Hall. Not unfitly Michael Drayton in his *Endimion and Phoebe* speaks of it as the plot 'where all the Muses be imparadis'd.'

'A guess,' it will be said. Yes, guess with a cir-

---

* Probably not before 1572. Sir Henry was confined in the Tower for some months after September 1571. Page-service, as in Drayton's case, might begin at a very early age and might continue until 'about eighteen,' which was the age of the girl-page, Bellario, in *Philaster*, and the page in the *New Way to Pay Old Debts* marries at the end of the play. All Shakespeare's girl-pages are marriageable or married.

cumstance. If anything is to be made out about the processes which made Shakespeare what he was, it can only be by conjecture. Here at least is a fact. The Stratford legend has no fact to go upon, and it is utterly improbable. Moreover, the fact is a link in a circumstantial train. The last link connects Shakespeare with Southampton.

§ 14 POLESWORTH

Polesworth (Powlesworth, Pollesworth) is a large village in the extreme north of Warwickshire, where an angle of the county is projected between Staffordshire and Leicestershire. The distance from Stratford —travelling by way of Warwick, Coventry and Nuneaton—is about thirty-eight miles. As other parishes in its neighbourhood, until its assignment to the modern diocese of Birmingham, it was included in that of Lichfield*. Stratford was in Worcester diocese.

The parish, which now has some 5000 inhabitants, was formerly more extensive, and within its limits contained, as Dugdale writes, nine 'villages and places of note,' besides Polesworth. The village is charmingly situated and retains much of its rural and ancient character, though its neighbourhood is defaced by the chimneys and collieries of Wilne-

* The Episcopal Register of Lichfield for the last half of the sixteenth century unfortunately contains only institutions to benefices in the diocese. There are no wills of the Polesworth Gooderes in the Lichfield Probate Office. Polesworth parish register begins in 1631.

cote, which is now a separate parish, formed in the last century out of the civil parishes of Tamworth and Polesworth. Wilnecote has a population about equal to that of Polesworth.

In medieval times the place was called Polesworth in Arderna. It was in the heart of the ancient forest of Arden. To 'cleere Ankor,' the river which flows through the village, Drayton dedicates the 13th *Amour* of his *Sonnets* (1594):

> 'Fayre *Arden*, thou my *Tempe* art alone,
> And thou, sweet *Ankor*, art my *Helicon*.'

'Polesworth,' says Professor Oliver Elton in his *Michael Drayton*, 'now consists chiefly of a street of ruddy-roofed, black-and-white cottages with the church and adjoining vicarage. Under the bridge crawls Drayton's river, the Ancor, as if in its sleep, like one of his own sluggish alexandrines. It is navigable by boats, upwards and downwards, for some distance, and winds among thick reeds, meadowsweet and willow into the Tame.'

The principal features of the place are its church, school and vicarage, all of which in their origin were a legacy of the Abbey of Benedictine nuns, founded in the reign of Stephen and dedicated to St Edith*.

The nuns surrendered their house to the King in January 1539: they had spent considerable

---

* According to a legendary history, cited in full in Dugdale's *Monasticon*, the abbey was founded by a Saxon king, Egbryght, at a place 'in the forest of Ardurne that was callyd Trensale, under a revar that was callyd Ancur, upon a depness of watur callyd Pollysworth.'

PLATE III

POLESWORTH CHURCH   FROM THE VICARAGE GARDEN

sums in the attempt to get a reprieve. Their expulsion was a sad business, moving to commiseration even the hard hearts of the Commissioners. Their letter to Lord Cromwell, dated July 28, 1537, deserves quotation, if only for its mention of the monastic school, which apparently survived the Dissolution, and conjecturally may have been the very scene of Shakespeare's schooling. They write that the Abbess, Alice Fitzherbert, was 'reputed to be a vertuouse woman and a gudd housewyffe and of great age,' and that many of the nuns were old, impotent and friendless.

'As we thinke, ye shall not speke in the preferment of a better Nonnery, nor of better women. And in the towne of Pollesworth are xliii tenements and never a plough but one: the resydue be artificers, laborers and vitellers and lyve in effect by the said house, and the repayre and resorte that ys made to the gentylmens children and sudjournentes that ther doo lyf to the nombre of xxx^{ti} and sometyme xl^{ti} and moo, that ther be right vertuously brought upp. And the Towne and Nonnery standith in a hard soile and barren ground, and to our estymacions, yf the Nonnery be suppressed, the towne will shortely after fall to ruyne and dekaye, and the people therin to the nombre of vi or vii^{xx} score persones are nott unlike to wander and to seke for their lyvyng.'

The site of the Abbey, with the lordship or manor of Polesworth and all the Abbey demesne, was sold in 1544 to Francis Goodere, a citizen of London, whose family had been long settled at Hadley in Hertfordshire. On his death the Polesworth estate

passed to his son, Sir Henry. Either Francis or
Henry destroyed the cloister buildings, and with
the materials erected a manor-house which occupied the site of the modern vicarage. The manor-
house was demolished about sixty years ago. A
photograph, taken before its destruction, shows
it as a building with an Italian front of the eighteenth century. Internally it was a rambling and
inconvenient structure, evidently preserving the
arrangements of a Tudor house. One feature of it
remains in the present vicarage. A fine fireplace
of arched stone occupies a wide space in the western
wall of the drawing-room, and in the spandrels
there is carved the Goodere rebus, a partridge with
an ear of corn in its bill. Some remains of the
monastic cloister survive in the vicarage garden.
The nave of the church has on its north side a fine
row of Norman arches—the two middle ones are
modern 'restoration'—with a semi-Norman clere-
story above. Both before and after the Dissolution
it served as the parish church. The chancel, which
had been the nuns' church, was destroyed or
dilapidated when the house was built. Perhaps as
a roofless relic it survived in Shakespeare's time:
possibly he had it in mind when, in the lovely
73rd Sonnet, he wrote the line

'Bare ruin'd choirs, where late the sweet birds
sang.'

One other part of the monastic buildings remains
—the picturesque gatehouse which, with the two-

storied wing adjoining it, presents a long 'tottered' front to the village street. The present vicar, the Rev. A. T. Corfield, with his own careful hands, and without 'restoration,' has adapted the upper floor of this building to the uses of a parish club room. I think that it is no unwarrantable stretching of the imagination to suppose that the room on this upper floor was used for the Abbey schoolroom. Monastic schools were necessarily external to the cloister: often they were located over or next to the gate*.

Mr A. F. Leach, in his *English Schools at the Reformation* (pp. 15–19), points out that a good many schools maintained by monasteries, chantries or gilds survived the Dissolution and the reign of Edward VI: but they were mostly schools provided by trusts which the monastery, etc. only administered, and at Polesworth there was no trust. In towns the maintenance of schools, after the dissolution of the trustee bodies, devolved on the corporation, which thenceforward appointed and paid the master. Such was the case at Stratford, Nuneaton, Solihull and Coventry. The school was then kept in some old building—chapel, hospital, a disused part of the church: 'a pedant that keeps

---

* I may cite the case of the schoolhouse which formerly existed in my own College, Jesus, Cambridge, which is the successor of a Benedictine nunnery dissolved in 1496. Whether the nuns kept a school, or not, I do not know: they certainly took in girls as boarders. Soon after 1500 a boys' school existed in the College, and it was placed partly over the gate of entrance, partly in the adjoining wing.

Polesworth

a school i' the church' was a familiar character in
Shakespeare's day. At Polesworth the chancel of
the church was destroyed soon after the Dissolution,
and it was contrary to the practice of the time to
use the parochial part of the church, *i.e.* the still-
existing nave, for school purposes. Polesworth had
no corporation and, if the very large Abbey school
was to be preserved and maintained in any sort,
it could only be done by the Gooderes, who in-
herited the responsibilities, as they did the estates,
of the nuns. That they did undertake the responsi-
bility in the case of the school I make little doubt:
and their reason for preserving the gatehouse
range, when they destroyed the other buildings of
the Nunnery, was that the school should be kept in
it, as it had been kept by the nuns.

There is the best reason for believing that the
present Nethersole School of Polesworth has a
continuous connection with a pre-existing school.
The founder, Sir Francis Nethersole (1587–1659),
came of a Kentish family. He was a Fellow of
Trinity, Cambridge, and at one time Public Orator
of the University. In middle life he was a Member
of Parliament, was deeply engaged in the affairs of
the Elector Palatine, and was knighted in 1619.
He married Frances Goodere, daughter of the
second Sir Henry who died without male issue,
and was grandniece of the first. In 1655 Sir Francis,
'at the special instance of his wife, who bore a great
affection to the Town, in regard it had been possest
by her Family from her Great-grandfather's time,

PLATE IV

POLESWORTH ABBEY

UPPER FLOOR OF THE GATEHOUSE RANGE

erected a convenient fabric of stone therein for a Schoolhouse, in the front whereof both his own and her arms were cut*.' The school, for girls as well as boys, still exists on the south side of the street, opposite the Nunnery gatehouse. Above its entrance is the inscription,

SOLI DEO GLORIA
SCHOLA PAUPERUM
PUERORVM PUELLARVM.

That what Nethersole did was to endow an already existing school, providing it with a new building and creating a trust for its control, is clear. By Mr Heaton, the clerk to the Nethersole governors, I am told: 'I have in my possession a copy of Sir Francis Nethersole's Grant to Trustees and Declaration to Charitable Uses of all his property in Polesworth, dated March 10, 1655, from which it is clear that there were at that date Schoolhouses and Schools and Teachers assigned to the same, viz. Francis Allen and Esther Barwell, and provision made for the apprenticing of poor children to trades.' As it is stated that Lady Nethersole's affection to Polesworth arose from her family's possession of the town from her great-grandfather's time, it is probable that Francis Goodere carried on the school from the time when he entered on the Nunnery estates, in or soon after 1544.

The schools established in the middle and latter part of the sixteenth century were almost exclusively

* Dugdale's *Warwickshire*.

for boys: with the education of girls, unless they were of good social position, that age did not concern itself. Nunnery schools in many cases provided for young boys as well as girls*. The Nethersole trust, providing for both girls and boys, was exceptional. I make no doubt that in that respect it perpetuated the system of the Abbey school, as the

A MASTER AND HIS CLASS OF BOYS AND GIRLS

Gooderes had already done. It is to be noted that schoolmaster Holofernes taught girls as well as boys. This was not the case at Corporation schools: but in the families of gentlefolk the tutor might teach boys and girls together. The picture above shows such a mixed class.

If one may infer from the examples of other Warwickshire schools, *e.g.* Stratford, Nuneaton and Warwick, the teaching was commonly supplied by

* See Miss Power's *Medieval English Nunneries*, pp. 263-264.

Shakespeare in North Warwickshire

a local parson. The 'chaplains' of Polesworth in Shakespeare's young days were John Atkyns (1557–1578) and John Savage (1578–1583). It is likely that Atkyns was Drayton's 'mild tutor.' Savage combined his duties with those of master at Sutton Coldfield school, where Robert Burton was perhaps his pupil. He was very likely related to a man of the same names, 'of the Inner Temple,' to whom Drayton addressed his fourth Ode (1606).

§ 15 SHAKESPEARE IN NORTH WARWICKSHIRE

But why Polesworth rather than Stratford? Of one place, as of the other, there is no mention in anything that Shakespeare wrote. At least we know that at Stratford he was born, for some time lived, and there died. Take Stratford out of the story and, apart from London, what remains?

'Patient investigation,' says Sir Sidney Lee, 'which has been in progress for more than two hundred years, has brought together a mass of biographical detail which far exceeds that accessible of any poet contemporary with Shakespeare.' Is it even so? Is our knowledge of Sidney, Spenser, Jonson, so small? Investigation has indeed laid bare to us in profusion the conditions of bourgeois life in Stratford. Quite respectable monographs might be, and have been, written on the lives of Stratford citizens who were neighbours and possible acquaintances of the William of Henley Street or

Shakespeare in North Warwickshire

the Shakespeare of the New Place. I suppose that there is no town in England which affords more ample witness of the manners and daily doings of its ordinary inhabitants in the days of Elizabeth and James. But though the picture is so full and vivid, the one figure which should dominate it is missing. In that lively scene there is as little chance of detecting the Poet-Dramatist as there is of discovering a portrait of Milton in a Teniers group of drinking boors. Wordsworth in his poetry is as communicative about himself as Shakespeare is reticent. But supposing that all that we knew of Wordsworth's *extra*-literary life were that he was the son of a Cumberland land-agent, received his first schooling in his native town, married a north-country woman whom he had known in youth, and settled and died in the Lake Country, what sort of picture should we have of his initiation and culmination in poetry? After ransacking Cockermouth for evidences of his parentage and environment we should be forced to the conclusion that, not in that utter nakedness, but in a world containing such places and people as Cambridge, Alfoxden and Lord Lonsdale the poet's soul had been fostered. At Stratford we know that books were few, that such education as a boy could get between the ages of seven and thirteen was meagre, and that the occupations of the burghers were not of a kind to interest them in literary matters. At Polesworth, on the surest evidence, we know that there were to be found books, a society of gentlefolk exceptionally

interested in literature, an education that encouraged poetic gifts, and patronage of budding
genius when schooldays were done. And that all
these were to be had so cheaply was Alderman
John's comfortable reflection.

But that is not all. We have seen that in his plays
Shakespeare has hardly a hint of familiarity with
Stratford and its neighbourhood. Of North Warwickshire, and particularly of the region round
about Polesworth, in an incidental way he has a
good deal to say.

Of course, in the absence of allusion to South
Warwickshire the Traditionalists take refuge in the
Cotswold Hills and Gloucestershire. What does
Shakespeare know about the Cotswolds? That there
was coursing there—a fact which all the world
knew. 'Will Squele, a Cotswold man, is noticed as
one of Shallow's friends.' So also was little John
Doit of Staffordshire, and the Staffordshire border
is close to Polesworth and a long way from the
Cotswolds. But in the Second Part of *Henry IV*
Shakespeare undoubtedly locates Justice Shallow
in Gloucestershire. Sir Sidney Lee can be 'very
precise' where Dogberry would say 'there is no
need of such vanity.' It so happens that there is a
place, the name of which in the Quarto (1600) and
First Folio text of the *Taming of the Shrew* is printed
Wincot: and there is a place, mentioned in the
Second Part of *Henry IV*, which in Quarto and Folio
is spelt *Woncot* or *Woncote*. Most editors, following
Malone's lead, have 'unwisely adopted' the spelling

73

Shakespeare in North Warwickshire

Wincot in the latter passage, thereby identifying the two places*. Not so Sir Sidney Lee.

'When the justice's factotum, Davy, asked his master to countenance William Visor of Woncot against Clement Perkes of the Hill the allusions are unmistakable to persons and places within the dramatist's personal cognisance. The Gloucestershire village of Woodmancote, where the family of Visor, or Vizard, has flourished since the sixteenth century, is still pronounced Woncot. The adjoining Stinchcombe Hill (still familiarly known to natives as "The Hill") was in the sixteenth century the home of the family of Perkes.'

The conjunction of the name *Woncot* with a place called 'the Hill' is surely wonderful 'out of all hooping.' But it might be suggested that 'Hills' existed both in Monmouth and Macedon, as well as elsewhere, and that Perkes is a common surname, instances of which are to be found in Warwickshire and other parts†. There is the further 'obvious reference' that in the Cotswolds red wheat was sown 'at an unusually early season of the agricultural year' which, of course, tallies with the order given to Davy to sow the headland with

* How indifferent or careless about the spelling of place-names Shakespeare's printers were is shown by the variant spellings Coltshold, Cotsale, Cotsall, Cotshall and Cotsole. In the First Folio text of *Macbeth* there are the spellings Byrnam, Byrnan, Birnane, Byrname, and Forres is printed *Soris*.

† The name of Perkes, or Perks, crops up at Stratford (Halliwell-Phillipps, *Outlines*, ii, p. 211) and at Coventry (Dormer Harris in the Index to vol. iv of the *Coventry Leet Book*, E.E.T.S.). My local knowledge does not entitle me to question the accuracy of the statement that the name Visor, 'or Vizard,' was known at Woodmancote in the sixteenth century.

74

Shakespeare in North Warwickshire

'red lammas': but red wheat and the time for sowing it were perhaps not unknown in other parts of England. Where and what is the Gloucestershire Woncot? It is a hamlet in the parish of Dursley, about fifty-four miles distant from Stratford. Imagine William, schoolboy or apprentice, trudging this distance, to and fro—on what visit? So far as we can judge from the plays, Gloucestershire was a strange county to Shakespeare. The only places in it which he mentions are Berkeley, Ciceter and Tewkesbury, and in his references to all three he simply follows the authority of Holinshed. In *Richard II* Northumberland, in the 'high wild hills' of Cotswold, speaks for Shakespeare when he says,

'I am a stranger here in Gloucestershire.'

Why Shakespeare chose to make Shallow a Gloucestershire man is a mystery. The right time for his appearance was obviously when Prince Hal was marching through Gloucestershire to Shrewsbury, and Falstaff might conveniently have taken that route and visited the justice, either going or returning. But to Shallow we are not introduced in the First Part of *Henry IV*. The first that is heard of him is in Act III, Scene 2 of the Second Part, when Falstaff comes to Gloucestershire, of all unlikely counties, to raise soldiers for the war in Yorkshire. When the fighting is over Falstaff asks leave to go through Gloucestershire, and presently says, 'I'll through Gloucestershire, and there will I visit Master Robert Shallow, esquire: I have him already

75

tempering between my finger and my thumb, and shortly will I seal with him.' A long journey for the knight to undertake!

Whatever the motive for planting the Shallow of *Henry IV* in Gloucestershire, Shakespeare very soon forgot about it, and unmistakably transfers him to Warwickshire. How else should his man, Davy, talk familiarly to him of Hinckley fair? Hinckley, in Leicestershire, is thirty-two miles from Stratford and fully forty from the near end of the Cotswolds. It is barely twelve from Polesworth.

But then the First Folio text of the same play presents a difficulty in this scrap of dialogue:

'*Shallow.* How a good yoke of bullocks at Stamford fair?
Silence. By my troth, I was not there.
Shallow. Death is certain. Is old Double of your town living yet?'

Cousin Silence's travels do not extend beyond his own neighbourhood. He certainly never attended Stamford fair, nor was it of the least consequence to him or to Shallow what price bullocks would fetch there. Stamford is distant some forty miles from the nearest edge of Warwickshire, and twice as far from the Cotswolds. But turn to the Quarto of 1600, which has higher critical value than the Folio text. The place is not Stamford, but Samforth, a name unknown to gazetteers. Something being clearly amiss, Heminge and Condell or the actors ventured the unhappy emendation 'Stamford.' 'Samforth,' I take it, is a mistake for 'Tamworth,' which is four miles distant from Polesworth. From Kelly's Directory (1924) I learn that 'A chartered fair, granted by Queen Elizabeth, chiefly for the sale of *cattle* and horses is held at Tamworth annually on July 27.' If I had a mind to be 'curious,' I would remark that Lammas day actually falls on August 1!*

Take Wincot, otherwise Wilnecote or Wilmecote. There is a place so named, where Robert Arden, Shakespeare's maternal grandfather, lived, farmed and owned land. He died before Shakespeare was born, but his widow continued to live there until her death in 1580. Its *name* was perhaps suggested to Shakespeare by the family connection: but it could hardly be the *place* mentioned in *Merry Wives* and the Second Part of *Henry IV*. Halliwell-Phillipps (*Outlines*, II, p. 307) describes it as

'a very minute and secluded hamlet in the parish of Clifton Chambers, and at about four miles from the poet's native town. It is described by Atkyns [in his *Gloucestershire*] in 1712 as then containing only two houses.... It is extremely unlikely that here was to be found an alehouse of any kind, and

* Tamworth is mentioned in *Richard III* (v, 2. 13). Holinshed has a curious story that the Earl of Richmond (Henry IV), on the eve of Bosworth Field, when his army was marching to Tamworth, lost his way at night, and after wandering hither and thither without hearing company, spent the night at a very little village about three miles from Tamworth, and next day made his way to Atherstone, where Lord Stanley was then abiding. Bramcote, where Holinshed spent his last years, is about three miles from Tamworth and not far from Atherstone. Local tradition perhaps fixed the scene of the incident there. Shakespeare makes the interview with Stanley happen on Bosworth Field.

there appears to be nothing beyond the mere name
to warrant conjectures of this being the hamlet
mentioned by Shakespeare.'

It is safe to say that it had no 'third, or fourth, or
fifth borough.'

But there is another Wincot, or Wilnecote, a far
more important place, which until the nineteenth
century was partly contained in the parish of
Polesworth. Close to it is Pooley Hall, also in
Polesworth parish, where Sir Thomas Cokain impaled a park which probably contained deer, and
may (or may not) have suggested Falstaff's deer-
stealing adventure. A descendant of Sir Thomas,
Sir Aston Cokain, had no question that this Wincot
was the scene of Christopher Sly's tippling. In a
poetical epistle (1658) addressed to his neighbour,
'Mr Clement Fisher of Wincott,' he writes:

'*Shakespeare* your *Wincot*-ale hath much renown'd
That fox'd a Beggar so (by chance was found
Sleeping) that there needed not many a word
To make him to believe he was a Lord:
But you affirm (and in it seem most eager)
'Twill make a Lord as drunk as any Beggar.
Bid *Norton* brew such Ale as *Shakespeare* fancies
Did put *Kit Sly* into such Lordly trances:
And let us meet there (for a fit of gladness)
And drink ourselves merry in sober sadness.'

Here is another indication that Shakespeare
forgot that he had made Shallow a Gloucestershire
man, and that he did not associate him with the
neighbourhood of Stratford. Master Silence, his
cousin and seemingly a neighbour, took exception

Shakespeare in North Warwickshire

to Pistol's salutation of Falstaff as one of the greatest men in the realm, and considered that Goodman Puff of Barson better deserved that description, as being the fattest man within the area of his knowledge. Barson is the local pronunciation of Barston, as Marson, in Warwickshire, is of Marston. The place is near Hampton-in-Arden, some fourteen miles distant from Polesworth, rather further from Stratford, and quite a long way from the Cotswold Hills.

The abiding-place of old John Naps of Greece is full of suggestion, but I doubt that the old gentleman had none of the Hellenic culture which his address, as it is spelt in the Quarto and First Folio, would imply. I make small doubt that Halliwell's conjecture, 'Greete,' is right. Greete is the name of a place on the north-western margin of the county, near Birmingham. Sir Sidney Lee writes: 'Greece may well be a misreading of Greet, a hamlet by Winchcombe in Gloucestershire, not far removed from Stratford' (it is actually twenty-three miles distant). 'According to local tradition Shakespeare was familiar with Greet, Winchcombe and *all*' (italics mine) 'the villages in their neighbourhood. He is still credited with the authorship of a local jingle, "Dirty Gretton, dingy Greet",' etc. The worthlessness of this 'tradition' is shown by the fact that 'dingy' is a modern word, not to be found in Johnson's *Dictionary*, and first appearing, as a provincialism, about 1750.

Shakespeare's Road to London

I have pointed out that in none of his plays dealing with English scenes does Shakespeare show any acquaintance with places on the Stratford-London road. The evidence of those plays does show a decided familiarity with the road between North Warwickshire and London. In the greater part of its course that road follows the route of the old Watling Street. It was the road by which Johnson, the editor, and Garrick, the actor, of Shakespeare's plays, travelled from Lichfield, 'riding and tying,' on their way to London. It was also the road taken by Drunken Barnabee in his celebrated *Itinerarium* (written *c.* 1638). It is worth while noting the route which he followed and the places that he stopped at.

Travelling on foot, he supped at Lichfield, next day crossed into Warwickshire, and before night got to Meriden. Next day, going by Coventry, he reached Dunchurch, a resort of highwaymen, but 'safe he sings whose purse is empty.' Early next morning he 'boused' at Daintree (Daventry), got a lift in a carrier's wagon at Weedon, and caroused all night (Tuesday) with a B.A. at Tosseter (Towcester). Thence he proceeded by Stony Stratford, Brickhill, Dunstable to Redburn, in Herts, 'where were Players,' and there apparently stopped the night. Then, by St Albans, Barnet and Highgate, he gets to the Lion Inn at Islington, and so, on the following morning, makes his way to London.

80

Shakespeare's Road to London

John Taylor, 'the water-poet,' in his *Penniless Pilgrimage* describes the journey which he took in 1618 by the same road, but in a reverse direction. Starting from Aldersgate on Tuesday, July 14, he reached Islington the first night, St Albans on the next, Stony Stratford on Thursday, and on Friday, passing through Towcester and Daventry, he camped for the night on Dunsmore Heath. He reached Coventry on Saturday and stayed there with 'Doctor Holland' until the following Tuesday, and then, through Sutton Coldfield, continued his travel to Lichfield. He carefully mentions all the inns at which he was entertained—all to be recommended, except the Horseshoe at Daventry.

Let us suppose that on his first journey to London Shakespeare started from somewhere near Polesworth: perhaps, in one or other direction, he travelled the same road more than once before he settled at Stratford. Travel was slow, and there were many stopping-places, even though he did not trudge as Barnabee did. The places which he mentions are all points in travel or in the march of soldiers. Most of them are places where Barnabee and Taylor stayed the night.

He would join the Watling Street not far from Wincot and, following it in a S.E. direction, would pass near Hinckley, two miles distant on his left. In a short day's journey he would reach Coventry, the famousest town in the shire, and frequently mentioned in the Plays. From Coventry he had the choice of three roads. He might take the road to

Shakespeare's Road to London

Rugby, whence Dr Caius' servant, Jack, took his eponym: or he might go over Dunsmore Heath (*Henry VI*, C, v, 1. 3) to Dunchurch: but, as the Heath was beset with highwaymen, it is likely that he would go by Southam to Daventry (both places in the same scene of *Henry VI*, and Daventry also in *Henry IV*, A, iv, 2. 51)*. Next he would pass Stony Stratford (*Richard III*, v, 4. 2) on his way to St Albans (many times mentioned). He makes mention of a red-faced innkeeper at Daventry and another 'host' at St Albans who sacrificed a shirt to equip Falstaff's regiment.

It may be argued that, as the London-Coventry road was the regular route of communication with the north-western parts of England, Shakespeare's familiarity with the stopping-places on it does not necessarily imply that he travelled by it. I only remark that he shows no acquaintance with it beyond Tamworth. If allusions in the Plays be an indication of highways known to him in travel, the only one, besides the Coventry road, which he was certainly acquainted with, was that to Windsor, as is shown by his mention of Brentford, Colnbrook, Staines, Maidenhead, Old Windsor and Eton: westward his knowledge ends at Reading. He knew that Gadshill and Rochester were on the Dover

---

* Daintree, Dunsmore and Southam are all in the *True Tragedy* scene corresponding to that in the Third Part, but Daintree and Dunsmore are transposed. As the names are not derived from Holinshed, I conclude that this part of the *True Tragedy* was written by a Warwickshire man, *i.e.* by Shakespeare, not Marlowe.

road, from information perhaps supplied by carriers and travellers frequenting Southwark inns. On the Southampton road he mentions Basingstoke, but the absence of any other Hampshire place-names suggests that he did not visit the Earl of Southampton at Titchfield. With places on the Great North Road and on the Norwich road I should suppose that he had no acquaintance. Nothing in the Plays suggests that he travelled with an acting company, but it is possible that he did so.

§ 17 MICHAEL DRAYTON

I hold that it is more than probable that Shakespeare at some early age was a page in Sir Henry Goodere's household: that he received his schooling at Polesworth: and that that school in his day was carried on in the same place where it existed in the monastic time—the old, unaltered room on the upper floor of the gatehouse range, about a hundred yards from the Hall. Possibly he slept in one of the smaller rooms on the lower floor*.

But I do not romance about the place, as Stratford school has been romanticised. He may, very likely, have learnt his 'absey' from a horn-book at Stratford. Simply we do not know: there is no shred of evidence to warrant even a surmise. To

---

* The porter's lodge is still to be seen next the archway of the gatehouse. Until a page was promoted to be a 'gentleman usher' the quarters customarily assigned to him were at or near the porter's lodge. In Massinger's *New Way to Pay Old Debts* Lord Lovel, addressing the page, Tom Allworth, says, 'Art thou scarce manumised from the porter's lodge?'

prove the superiority of Stratford school a good deal
has been made of the fact that the master received
from the Corporation the unusually high wage of
£20 *per annum*. Nevertheless, the masters made
haste to exchange their posts for better ones:
between 1569 and 1582 there were at least five
successive holders of the office.

In the sixteenth century Warwickshire was well
provided with schools. The most famous was that
of Coventry. The town of Warwick maintained a
school of considerable note. Robert Burton, of the
Anatomy of Melancholy, was taught successively at
Sutton Coldfield and at Nuneaton. There were
schools at Birmingham, Solihull, Atherstone and
Rugby. All of these schools were established shortly
after the Dissolution: most of them took the place
of pre-existing chantry or gild schools. Shakespeare,
for aught we know, may have attended any one of
them: if he did, the costs of his board and teaching
must have been supplied by some richer person
than John Shakespeare, who could get a free education for his boy at Stratford.

Of course, no Elizabethan school kept any
register of admissions: unless an author himself or
somebody nearly contemporary with him gives us
the information, it is impossible to say how he got
his education. Therefore it is not surprising that
of the list of sixty-eight (p. 54) in the case of ten—
Shakespeare makes an eleventh—there is no record
of the place of education. Among these ten there
is one who in family antecedents, local associations

Michael Drayton

and literary career inevitably challenges comparison with Shakespeare—the Warwickshire poet, Michael Drayton.

Drayton was born in 1563, one year before Shakespeare, at Hartshill, a small place between Nuneaton and Atherstone, and close to Oldbury, where the Polesworth nuns had a cell and lands which passed with their other estates to the Goodere family. His grandfather was a butcher and, according to Aubrey, his father exercised the same trade. At an early age he was received into the household of Sir Henry Goodere of Polesworth, apparently as a page. It does not appear that he attended any school, unless it were the school supported by Sir Henry. To Sir Henry he expressly acknowledges that he owed the most part of his education. In the delightful Elegy addressed to his friend, Henry Reynolds, he describes how his 'mild tutor' smilingly encouraged him in his aspiration to be a poet, reading with him first 'Mantuan,' then Virgil's *Eclogues*, and ending, it would seem, with Chaucer, Gower and later English poets. It was Sir Henry who introduced him to his patroness, Lucy, Countess of Bedford. He witnessed Sir Henry's will in 1595. All through life his memory went back to the kindly society of Polesworth Hall. The 'Idea' celebrated in his Sonnets was Sir Henry's younger daughter, Anne, afterwards wife of Sir Henry Rainsford of Clifton Chambers, near to Stratford. In his *Polyolbion* the first syllable of the river name, Ancor, suggests to him her Christian

85

name, as the first of her surname, Godere, recalls the first of Godiva, the lady of Coventry. In one of his Elegies, addressed to the younger Sir Henry Goodere, he describes how he used to sit—doubtless at the same fireplace that still exists in the drawing-room at the vicarage—listening to the music of John Hewes, the Welsh harper, which

> 'oft at Polesworth by the fire
> Hath made us gravely merry.'

Except for the tradition of the 'merry meeting' with Shakespeare and Jonson, just before Shakespeare's death, there is no positive evidence to tell us what fellowship there may have been between the two Warwickshire poets. In his well-known reference to Shakespeare (1627) he speaks of his 'comic vein' in a way which suggests that he knew or appreciated little of the great tragedies. Coming after his warm eulogy of 'the brave translunary things' of Marlowe, his commendation of Shakespeare's 'strong conception' seems to us inadequate. In truth, Drayton, who had unsuccessfully attempted stage-writing himself, was incapable of appreciating high dramatic invention. His tribute to Marlowe was perhaps the due paid to *Hero and Leander*, which was the inspiration and model of his own *Endimion and Phoebe*. Perhaps we should assume that he was not particularly well acquainted with Shakespeare in the days when both of them were in London. If his written reminiscences do not take him back to the schoolfellow of his boyhood, that

PLATE V

DRAYTON'S FIREPLACE IN POLESWORTH VICARAGE

Michael Drayton

is what might be expected. Edmund Spenser and
Lancelot Andrewes were contemporaries at school
(Merchant Taylors', London) and at Cambridge
(Pembroke Hall): the circumstance is only known
to us from school and University records. Fulke
Greville, in his *Life of Sir Philip Sidney*, states that
he 'lived with him (Sidney) and knew him from a
child': but he omits to mention that they were at
Shrewsbury school together, and that they entered
that school on the same day.

Though we need not attach much credit to the
story of the 'merry meeting,' there is reason for
thinking that in late life Drayton and Shakespeare
renewed the acquaintance of their youth, if not at
New Place, at the residence of Sir Henry Rainsford
at Clifton Chambers, a hamlet situated just over the
Gloucestershire border, two miles or so from Stratford. Sir Henry survived Lady Anne, Drayton's
'Idea,' and his death in 1622 wrung from Drayton
an affectionately disconsolate Elegy:

'Who had seen
His care of me, wherever I have been...
He would have sworn that to no other end
He had been born but only for my friend.'

The kindly relations of the poet with the family
of Clifton Chambers did not cease with the death
of Sir Henry. Writing to his friend, William Drum-
mond, from Clifton Chambers in 1631, a few months
before his own death, Drayton says that he is
stopping at a knight's house in Gloucestershire, 'to
which place I yearly use to come in the summer

time to recreate myself and to spend some two or three months in the country.' The knight was the younger Henry Rainsford, son of his old flame, 'Idea.'* These visits began when Shakespeare and the elder Rainsford were living, for in the fourteenth Song of *Polyolbion* (1613) he writes that Clifton Chambers has been 'many a time the Muses' quiet port.' Shakespeare, too, could hardly fail to know and visit the Rainsfords. His son-in-law, Dr John Hall, counted Lady Anne among his patients, and cured Drayton, whom he mentions as 'an excellent poet,' of a tertian fever. It is quite conceivable that Jonson, the friend of both poets, visited Stratford or Clifton Chambers on the occasion of his stay with the younger Sir Henry Goodere at Polesworth, which happened certainly not later than 1616.

§ 18 THE POLESWORTH CIRCLE

The north-east corner of Warwickshire, in the last quarter of the sixteenth century and the first of the seventeenth, was a very remarkable hive of literary activity, gathered about Polesworth Hall and the Goodere family. It may be questioned whether, within that half-century and in so limited an area, there could be counted, at any place outside London, so large a number of writers distinguished in their several lines—resident or visitors.

Bramcote Hall, now an old and substantial farm-house, is situated in Polesworth parish, less than a

* Elton, *Michael Drayton*, pp. 126-131.

mile from the church. It was the seat of the Burdet family, and in Shakespeare's youth was occupied by Thomas Burdet (d. 1603) whose monument in the neighbouring church of Seckington describes him as 'secretarius e secretioribus consiliis' to Queen Elizabeth. In his service at Bramcote, as steward of his estate, lived Raphael Holinshed, the chronicler, and there died in 1580. His great *Chronicles of England, Scotland and Ireland* had been published in 1578. Possibly he was known to the two pages, Drayton and Shakespeare. More likely his two stout volumes lay on some window seat in Polesworth Hall, and from them Drayton drew matter for his *Heroical Epistles* (1596) and Shakespeare for his early historical plays: but it was the second edition of the *Chronicles*, published in 1586, that supplied Shakespeare with materials for his later Histories.

It is likely that Thomas Lodge, whose story of *Rosalynde* supplied the plot of *As You Like It*, was a visitor at Polesworth Hall at a time when Drayton, but not Shakespeare, was there. Lodge adopted the pseudonym of Golde, and in that name is addressed by Drayton at the end of his *Endimion and Phoebe* (1595):

'And thou, my Goldey, which in Sommer dayes
Hast feasted us with merry roundelayes,
And when my Muse scarce able was to flye
Didst imp her wings with thy sweete Poesie.'

As Drayton was unmarried, 'us' must refer to some family with whom both were staying, and 'Sommer

The Polesworth Circle

dayes' points to a country house. In later life, as I have said, it was Drayton's habit to spend the summer months at Clifford Chambers, the married home of Anne Rainsford, daughter of Sir Henry Goodere. Lodge was absent from England on a voyage to the Canaries in 1589, during which he wrote *Rosalynde* (published in 1590), and again on a voyage to South America from August 1591 until the early part of 1593. If he visited Polesworth it was probably in the summer of 1593, and Drayton seems to have been there about that year (p. 103 *note*). Drayton's first successful venture in poetry, *Idea, the Shepherd's Garland*, appeared in that year. Shakespeare was no doubt in London, 'bumbasting' on the stage and correcting the proof-sheets of *Lucrece*.

Robert Burton was born in 1577 at Lindley, a small place in Leicestershire, just outside the Warwickshire border. In the *Anatomy* he speaks of 'Oldbury in the confines of Warwickshire, where I have often looked about me with great delight: at the foot of which hill I was born.' Oldbury, as I have mentioned, was part of the Goodere estate. Speaking of sites suitable for gentlemen's mansions he mentions Polesworth 'among places best to me known, upon the river Anker in Warwickshire.' He was a 'grammar scholar' successively at Sutton Coldfield and Nuneaton. The former place, he says, 'stands, as Camden notes, *loco ingrato et sterili*, but in an excellent air.' What says Shallow of his estate?

PLATE VI

POOLEY HALL, POLESWORTH

FROM THE RIVER ANCOR

The Polesworth Circle

'*Falstaff.* 'Fore God, you have here a goodly
dwelling and a rich.
Shallow. Barren, barren, barren; beggars all,
beggars all, Sir John: marry, good air.'

And at Sutton Coldfield there was actually 'a chace
of great extent' (Gough's *Camden*). And near it
there is actually a village called 'Hill.' Was Shallow,
then, a Sutton Coldfield squire, known to Shakespeare? I trow not.

In this same Polesworth parish there remains
another Hall, ancient and more dignified than
Bramcote, and like Bramcote, harbouring traditions
of books and their writers—Pooley Hall, which for
a century was possessed by some curious denizens
in the by-alleys of Tudor and Jacobean literature.
The estate of Pooley came into the possession of the
Cokain family in the reign of Henry IV: they were
also possessed of a large lordship at Ashbourne in
Derbyshire.

Pooley Hall, now the property and residence of
Colonel D'Arcy Chaytor, who has repaired and
recovered it from a semi-ruinous condition, exists
at the present day, materially and in appearance,
exactly as we may suppose that it presented itself
to Shakespeare, and therefore deserves a few words
of description. It is picturesquely seated on the
crown of a steep slope descending to the river
Ancor. The main part of the buildings, of red brick
with stone dressings, was erected by Sir Thomas
Cokain in or about 1508. The central and domi-
nating feature is a tower, 40 feet high, with walls

4 feet 6 inches thick, and capped by a battlemented
parapet. Though the residential parts of the man-
sion are not extensive and the Great Hall has
vanished, enough remains to indicate the scale of
comfort and luxury of the original design. Fine
oak panelling remains in certain of the upper floor
rooms, some of it elaborately carved. In the large
garret floor may be seen the massive timbers,
acutely pitched, which support the Gothic roof.
Near the house, and once connected with it by a
gallery on the first floor level, is a charming little
chapel with traceried windows, a good late-Per-
pendicular western door and octagonal bell-turret.

In Shakespeare's youth the lord of Pooley was
Sir Thomas Cokain, who died in 1592. He was a
'professed hunter,' and wrote a book (1590) entitled
*A Short History of Hunting, compyled for the delight of
Noblemen and Gentlemen.* His grandson, another
Thomas (1587–1638), married Anne, daughter of
Sir Edward Ashby of Willoughby-in-the-Wolds,
Notts, a good woman to whom Donne addressed
letters ('My Noblest Sister') which are printed in
Sir Edmund Gosse's *Life of Donne.* Thomas was a
crazy person who deserted his wife and family, hid
himself in London under the assumed name of
Brown, and was supposed to be engaged in com-
piling an English-Greek lexicon. His eldest son,
Sir Aston, born in 1608, succeeded to the Pooley
estate, but not to the Ashbourne property, in 1638.
He was the friend of Dugdale and Massinger. He
was author of various books of poems, a masque

PLATE VII

POOLEY HALL, POLESWORTH, WITH THE CHAPEL

FROM THE WEST

and two comedies, all of slight merit. Anthony à Wood says that he 'was esteemed of many an ingenious gentleman, a good poet, and a great lover of learning, yet by others a perfect boon-fellow, by which means he wasted all he had.' He was a 'compounder' for his devotion to the King's cause, and was furthermore fined as a 'popish delinquent.' He sold Pooley in 1683, shortly before his death.

Of the greater names of Ben Jonson and John Donne I have yet to speak.

§ 19 THE GOODERES

Sir Henry Goodere, Drayton's friend, born in 1534, was the elder son of that Francis Goodere who acquired Polesworth after the dissolution of the Abbey. He had a younger brother, William, who witnessed his will in 1595, and was father of the younger Sir Henry. This William was probably the writer of *The Voyage of the Wandering Knight*, translated out of the French of Jean de Cartigny. So far as we know, Sir Henry wrote nothing himself, but we have the testimony of Dugdale that he was 'a Gentleman much accomplisht and of eminent note in the Countie (*i.e.* Warwickshire) while he lived.' He married Frances, daughter of Henry Lowther and sister of Sir Richard Lowther, who took part in the Rising in the North (1570) and in the Catholic project, culminating in the Ridolfi plot of 1571, of marrying the Duke of Norfolk to Mary, Queen of Scots, and putting her on the throne.

93

The Gooderes

Goodere was also involved in the latter business, and was sent to the Tower in September 1571, but was released in 1572. From his prison in the Tower he wrote to Burleigh confessing at length the particulars of his communications in cipher with the Queen of Scots, the bishop of Ross and the Duke of Norfolk, and protesting his innocence of any treasonable designs. It does not appear that he was a declared Roman Catholic. He probably belonged to that large section of the gentry who resented the ultra-Protestant rule, and looked for a riddance of it in the succession of the Queen of Scots, but were not privy to the treasonable practices promoted to effect that end. He seems to have been introduced to Mary—perhaps when she was in the charge of his brother-in-law at Lowther Hall, more certainly when she was interned at Coventry in 1570—and he became devotedly attached to her person. In the spring of 1583 he was visited by John Somerville, a rash Warwickshire youth who proposed to go to London to shoot Queen Elizabeth. Goodere, if the scheme was communicated to him, was wise enough to have nothing to do with it: but he talked romantically of the captive Mary, and showed Somerville some buttons which she had given him as a token of her gratitude for his services and sufferings in her cause. He made his peace with Elizabeth, served under Leicester in Flanders in 1585, was knighted in 1586, and was a colonel in the Queen's bodyguard at Tilbury in 1588. He died at Polesworth on March 5, 1595, and the Polesworth estate passed

94

The Gooderes

to his elder daughter, Frances, and her husband, the second Sir Henry*.

Sir Henry Goodere, the younger, was born in 1571, probably at Monks Kirby, between Nuneaton and Rugby, where his father lived. In 1587 he matriculated as a Fellow-commoner at St John's, Cambridge (a circumstance worth remembering). In November 1592 he acted as one of the Commissioners appointed to enquire about recusants. In and after 1603 he was a regular attendant at the court of James, and in 1604 he addressed a letter to Cecil urgently petitioning for pecuniary assistance on the twofold ground of his expenses in the King's service and his uncle's sufferings in the cause of Mary, Queen of Scots. In recompense he was granted a small forfeited estate of £50 per annum, and was appointed a gentleman of the privy chamber. But his embarrassments continued until his death, March 18, 1627. He left four daughters, of whom the eldest, Lucy, married Sir Francis Nethersole.

Goodere himself wrote occasional verses on court topics, and others which are included in Coryat's *Crudities*—lame and 'conceited' they are. In 1611 we find him attending a 'philosophicall feast,' celebrated in rhyming Latin verses by Coryat, and

* Sir Henry had a town house in Coventry, and it appears that there, not at Polesworth, the meeting with Somerville took place. Drayton, in his *Hymne to his Ladies Birthplace*, says that his 'Idea' was born at Mich Park in Coventry. Possibly Shakespeare, as boy or master, attended Coventry school: if so, it was not when Philemon Holland was master there, for Holland did not take up his abode there until after 1595.

The Gooderes

among fellow-guests were John Donne, Hugh Holland and Inigo Jones. It is as the friend of Donne that he is best remembered. Beginning in 1600, Donne wrote to him weekly letters of the most intimate kind, forty of which are printed in Sir Edmund Gosse's *Life of Donne*. It was Goodere who introduced him to the notice of the Countess of Bedford. Donne was visiting Polesworth about Easter 1613. Goodere was also a friend of Jonson, who in his 85th Epigram (printed in the Folio of 1616) thanks him for a few days' hawking, presumably at Polesworth. In the 86th Epigram Jonson writes:

'When I would know thee, Goodyere, my thought
  looks
Upon thy well-made choice of friends and books:
Then do I love thee and behold thy ends
In making thy friends books, and thy books friends.'

As a friend of Jonson and Holland it is likely that he was personally acquainted with Shakespeare: but I do not know that there is any evidence of the connection. If, as seems likely, Shakespeare was a visitor, or possibly, as tutor or schoolmaster, was resident at Polesworth before his exit to London, Goodere may have known him there. It has to be remembered that there is no scrap of evidence for fixing 1586 as the year of Shakespeare's introduction to London. For all that we know it might be as late as 1590.

The Sonnets

Of all the problems which beset Shakespeare's early life, none is more problematical than that of his introduction to Southampton and early relations with him. In this field there is permissible scope for surmise, let the surmise only have some element of probability and some basis of fact.

Conjecture must needs touch the well-worn theme of the Sonnets and of the person addressed in the first series of them. Though the date of their publication was 1609, it will scarcely be contested that in composition they belong to the poetic, less-dramatic time of Shakespeare's output: that their elaborated language, harmonic cadences and cyclical involution of thought are of the time which produced *Venus* and *Lucrece*. The 126th Sonnet is reasonably interpreted as a dedication to the Lord of the writer's love of some 'written ambassage' which may very well be either of these poems—more probably *Lucrece*. In any case the allusion to the Sonnets by Francis Meres, as circulating in manuscript among private friends, is proof that at least some of them were written at a date earlier than 1598. It is fairly clear that the whole of the first series has reference to one individual who was not a woman: that he was adulated by some rival poet: that he was considerably younger than Shakespeare, and yet old enough to be wooed by women and to make his marriage a thing natural and desirable.

The Sonnets

In the 104th Sonnet, Shakespeare says of him that three years have passed since 'first your eye I eyed,' from which it is to be gathered that the intimacy was of some standing. Southampton, born in 1573, was nine years junior to Shakespeare, his age being twenty at the date when *Venus* was printed with a dedication to him.

The conditions fit Southampton so well that probably there would have been no thought of looking further for the inspirer of the Sonnets of the first series, but for the troublesome dedication by the publisher, 'T.T.,' *i.e.* Thomas Thorpe, which has started the incredible notion that in 'Mr W. H., the onlie begetter of these insuing sonnets,' the name of William Herbert, Earl of Pembroke, is disguised. If it were not for the players' dedication of the First Folio to him and his brother, Philip, we should be unaware that Shakespeare in his lifetime had been 'prosequuted' by him with any special favour. As the Earl of Pembroke was a boy of thirteen in 1593, it seems in the last degree unlikely that he was the 'fair man,' captivated by the 'dark woman,' and the too successful rival of the poet*. Sir Sidney Lee's theory that the 'begetter' was merely one of the publishing fraternity, who procured for Thorpe the privately circulated manuscript, is so far much more probable. But it leaves out of sight the significant word 'onlie,' which would have no applica-

* The evidence given by Mrs Stopes in *The Third Earl of Southampton*, pp. 42, 43, for the conclusion that 'Mr W. H.' cannot be identified with William Herbert, seems to me to put the matter beyond reasonable doubt.

tion to a trade middleman, and it ignores the yet more significant wish for 'that eternitie promised by our ever-living poet,' which can surely mean nothing else than a promise expressed in the published Sonnets. That promise of eternity is plainly written in Sonnet 18, and in Sonnet 19 the poet writes,

'My love shall in my verse ever live young.'

Let us look at the thing in the light of commonsense probability. 'W. H.,' whatever his actual name and initials were, is a literary thief. He hangs about the Southampton circle, and 'pecks up wit, as pigeons pease, and utters it again when God shall please.' There is money to be made out of anything that comes from the pen of Shakespeare, and 'W. H.' knows where to 'retail his wares.' 'T. T.' is well known as a receiver of stolen literary goods: Marlowe, Chapman, Jonson in turn fit his shopboard with true men's apparel. To him comes 'W. H.' with a lame story that the Sonnets are addressed to *him*—that he has a kind of copyright interest in them. As the displeasure of his patron is to be avoided, he has the best of reasons for pseudonymity. The honest broker benevolently smiles, as knowing well the source of these 'sugred sonnets.' The story fits his purpose well. At any hand it will not do to label his purchase 'late the property of the Right Honourable the Earl of Southampton,' or to indicate the channel by which it has been 'conveyed' to him. The dedication to the imaginary 'Mr W. H.' is a mere blind*.

It is likely that the composition of the Sonnets extended over several years. There is nothing in them to furnish a clue as to date, but the tone of the earliest makes it clear that the person addressed was barely entered on manhood. The strong personal feeling in them is something deeper than a conventional expression of devotion to a lordly patron, and savours more of the dedication of *Lucrece* than that of *Venus*. So I conjecture that these first Sonnets date from about 1594. The acquaintance of author and patron is then likely to have begun in the spring of 1591. Greene's *Groatsworth of Wit*, written just before his death in September 1592, breaks the seven years' silence in Shakespeare's life. From that splenetic attack we learn that at that time Shakespeare was 'bumbasting out' other men's blank verse, and as 'the only *Shake-scene* in a country,' was defrauding playwrights, such as Greene himself, of the credit due to their 'admired invention.' But Chettle, in December 1592, had discovered that Shakespeare had also 'a facetious grace in writing,' presumably of drama. For reasons which I shall state, I do not think that it was his excellence in the quality of

* This theory of the matter derives support from the similar case of *Ferrex and Porrex*. The publisher of the authorised edition of 1571 says that this tragedy was 'never intended by the authors thereof to be published: yet one W. G., getting a copy thereof at some young man's hand that lacked a little money and much discretion, about five years past put it forth much corrupted, neither of the authors being made privy.'

Southampton

actor that first introduced him to the notice of Southampton. It was a more personal link that brought them together.

§ 21 SOUTHAMPTON

Among the prisoners committed to the Tower in September 1571, for supposed complicity in the Ridolfi plot, was Henry Goodere, the elder: another was his brother-in-law, Richard Lowther, a Roman Catholic. On the same charge Henry Wriothesley, second Earl of Southampton (also a Roman Catholic), was imprisoned in the Tower from October 1571 to May 1573. Goodere was released in 1572. It is likely that he was known to the Earl before their arrest.

'Henry Goodere was examined on October 13, chiefly about Mary Stuart, but also about Southampton.... On July 9, 1572, there was a new examination of Henry Goodere, Henry Percy and the earl of Southampton.... Goodere said, "Being imprisoned in a tower, not past thirty foot from the tower where the earl of Southampton lieth, and of Henry Percy, sometimes walking in a little court that he used, at one time only did he speak to the Earl, and especially of the deliverance of the Earl. The Earl did once come towards this examinate with a joyful countenance, and said that he heard good news, and that my Lord of Leicester had sent him word that he should keep his promise to him. ...But Sir Henry Percy was often on the Leads when this examinate was at his book, and he does not know if the Earl talked to him." Sir Henry Percy said "he had often spoken with Mr Goodere, but only of their deliverance." Southampton himself, being examined, acknowledged that "he had talked with Sir Henry Percy and Mr Goodere on the Leads" etc.*'

The acquaintance, cemented in these unfortunate circumstances, was probably continued until the Earl's death in 1581. His son, Henry (Shakespeare's friend), who succeeded him as third Earl, was only eight years old when his father died. At the age of twelve he was entered as a Fellow-commoner at St John's College, Cambridge. Admissions at a very early age were not uncommon at the Universities in the sixteenth century. It is to be remembered that Southampton was a Roman Catholic. The oath taken at matriculation did not expressly involve renunciation of the Roman faith, but the obligation required in it to maintain the Protestant statutes was, no doubt, interpreted as including it. For this reason it was a common practice for a Roman Catholic to matriculate as *impubes*, *i.e.* under the age of fourteen, the matriculant of that age being exempted from oath-taking. For example, John Donne and his brother, Henry, sons of Roman Catholic parents, matriculated at Oxford at the ages of ten and eleven.

Southampton remained at Cambridge until he took the degree of M.A. in 1589. Henry Goodere, the younger, matriculated from the same college (St John's) as a Fellow-commoner in October 1587, at the age of sixteen. He was therefore contem-

* Mrs Stopes, *The Third Earl of Southampton*, pp. 512, 513.

porary there with Southampton for some two years, and as both belonged to the privileged class of Fellow-commoners, a considerable intimacy must have existed between them, and the literary interests of either of them are likely to have prolonged it in later years. In 1599 both of them were in Ireland with Essex, and to that circumstance may be attributed Shakespeare's unwonted enthusiasm in a matter of contemporary politics, as revealed by the Chorus in *Henry V*. Probably Goodere was the 'H. G.' who in 1618 produced a book called *The Mirrour of Majestie*, in which a page is devoted to the Earl of Southampton, and accompanying a picture of his arms are two copies of verses in his honour, one of them commending the union in him of Arts and Victory*.

In 1591 the first Sir Henry Goodere was getting old, as age went in the sixteenth century. He died four years later at the age of sixty-one. He had no son, and his nephew, who ultimately married his daughter, Frances, and succeeded him at Polesworth Hall, was a youth of twenty years. Drayton in boyhood had been fostered under his roof, had perhaps continued there as he advanced to manhood, and clearly remained on intimate terms with him†. To London it was inevitable that he, with

* As 'H. G.' Goodere has verses in Drayton's *Matilda* (1594), and to 'H. G.' Drayton dedicated his *Odes* in 1606.
† In the 12th Sonnet of his *Idea* (1602) Drayton, speaking of his infatuation for his mistress, presumably Anne Goodere, writes:
    ''Tis nine years now since first I lost my wit.'
This sonnet is not in the editions of 1594 and 1599. It is to be concluded that he was a visitor at Polesworth about 1593.

aspirations for poetry, should drift, and to London he went, much about the same time, we may suppose, as Shakespeare went. London in those days was as hard a stepmother to provincial genius as it showed itself later to Johnson and Chatterton. Drayton did not adventure himself there without the prospect of friendly help and patronage to advance him in his career. He writes: 'That excellent and matchless gentleman, Sir Henry Goodere, was the first cherisher of my Muse, which had been by his death left a poor orphan to the world, had he not before bequeathed it to the Lady Lucy, countess of Bedford.' To her he addresses several of his poems, and she was a notable patroness of poets and dramatists—Jonson, Donne, Chapman, Daniel of the number. We may guess that he arrived in London about the year 1591, which is the date of his first published poem, *The Harmony of the Church.* He tried his luck, unsuccessfully, in historical play-writing, was one of Henslowe's hacks, and his early work was much on the same lines as Shakespeare's—romance of the Ovidian pattern in *Endimion and Phoebe* and sonnets in *Idea's Mirrour* (both in 1594).

Something of the same kind must have happened to Shakespeare. It is hard to believe that he deserted wife and family without any definite prospect of obtaining maintenance for them. It is scarcely likely that a young man, possessed of no skilled occupation other than that of an apprentice in a fallen trade, with no better education than the elements which he had acquired as a child and had forgotten since in long untutored years, should adventure his inexperience in the keen competition of London. The Stratford apologist finds an 'illuminating parallel with Shakespeare' in the experiences of Richard Field, a tanner's son of Stratford, whose career showed that 'country breeding proved no bar to civic place and power,' inasmuch as he 'rose to the head of his profession' as a London Stationer. ''Tis all one, 'tis alike as my fingers is to my fingers.' Shakespeare failed to attain to civic place—even at Stratford. Field came to London in 1579 at the age of fifteen, served the usual seven years of apprenticeship there, and married the widow of his master, Vautrollier—avenues to success which were not open to Shakespeare.

He had no children born at Stratford after 1585. Whether he had any born to him in London or elsewhere we do not know. There is no ground for fixing his migration from Warwickshire in the year 1586 or in any other year between that and 1592. I have shown reason for thinking that his first and early journeys were between Polesworth and London. It is probable that, like Drayton, he went with introductions from the elder Goodere to friends in London. The younger Goodere had recently left Cambridge. If he were in London, what more natural than to make his Warwickshire friend acquainted with the friend whom he had known at Cambridge? Is it just possible that in the

31st Sonnet, where Shakespeare writes of 'lovers gone, who all their parts of me to thee did give,' he calls to mind the kind Warwickshire patron (dead in 1595) who transferred his 'part' in the poet to Southampton?

It was not the lure of the theatre which drew Shakespeare to London. Neither in the Sonnets nor in the dedications to the Poems does he indicate that his patron was in any way interested in the stage. The expression in Sonnet 110 has been tortured into a reference to his profession as an actor, but even so, it is an apology for it. Nor is it probable that the young Earl's interest in him began with the stage. In 1599, after his return from Ireland, it is recorded that Southampton and his friend, Roger Manners, Earl of Rutland, 'pass away the time merely in going to plays every day': but of his earlier addiction to stage performances nothing is known. Before 1599 he was the centre of a literary circle, several of whom dedicated their works to him, but none of them were dramatic*. *A Lover's Complaint*, though its ascription to Shakespeare has no better authority than that of the pirate publisher, Thomas Thorpe, may yet be a work of his pre-London days, separated by some years from *Venus*. I imagine that until 1594 his aspiration was to poetical romance. The first evidence that he was associated with an acting company comes from Greene's *Groatsworth of Wit* in 1592, and that he

* Mr Nichol Smith in *Shakespeare's England* (ii, pp. 199–201) gives a list.

was then newly recruited to the stage is evident from Greene's assault on him as an '*upstart* crow.' The 'pribbles and prabbles' told by the parish clerk of Stratford, that he 'was received into the playhouse as a serviture,' deserve as little credit as his other statement that he was apprenticed to a butcher and 'ran from his master.' The similar figment that his connection with the theatre began with holding horses at the playhouse door has just as little to recommend it. It has no earlier authority than the statement of Theophilus Cibber in his *Lives of the Poets* (1753). Its supposed pedigree is traced through Pope, Rowe and Betterton to the dubious paternity of Davenant: but it is odd that neither Pope nor Rowe thought it worthy of notice.

§ 22 WARWICKSHIRE SCENES IN
SHAKESPEARE'S YOUTH

I have said, and I am firmly convinced, that in his Plays Shakespeare never consciously delineated the individual features or characteristics of any contemporary. Shallow is the composite portrait of many Shallows known to him. I am equally convinced that, excepting places in or near London and Windsor, which were as familiar to his audiences as to himself, he is never at any pains to picture the actual localities in which his scenes are laid. When Edgar describes Dover cliffs he is really out of hearing of the sea and standing on even ground. Shakespeare's stage had no scenery to explain to the audience that the scene of the *Merchant* was laid in Venice, and he gives no description of its waterways to help them to realise that Venice was other in appearance than Ephesus or an un-named city in Illyria. So far let Stratford take comfort. If Shakespeare had chosen to lay any of his scenes in Stratford, he would have left his audience to entertain their unaided conjecture of its streets and buildings. But somehow he would have created the atmosphere of a small provincial town, as in his Venice he has created the atmosphere of merchant life and civic dignity. Somehow names of localities in the neighbourhood would have crept into his story, and he would have worked in details of his own observation of life in a petty town—small tradesmen and their wives, prentices and municipal dignitaries, such people as delighted Heywood and Middleton. People of that middle class are removed by him to rural regions, or London, or cities which are the counterparts of London.

But scenes of rural life, and especially those aspects of it which in the forest surroundings of such a place as Polesworth were most likely to be fresh in Shakespeare's recollection, are to be found in most of his early work, from *Venus* in 1593 down to *As You Like It*, *c*. 1600, and casual references to deer-hunting in that period of his writing are too numerous to be particularly mentioned. Such scenes and references disappear after 1600. In the later plays the scene is in ideal places—Welsh hills, Bohemian pastures, a Mediterranean island. The sound of the sea is in most of them, and the 'Heart of England' is forgotten.

The Two Gentlemen, *Love's Labour's Lost* and *Midsummer Night's Dream*, plays which most clearly present the woodland landscape, are all of them mentioned by Meres in his list of the Plays known to him when he wrote in 1598. There has never been any hesitation in regarding them as written exclusively by Shakespeare. But his fellows and their dramatic manager, Henslowe, did not commission him to write original plays until he had proved himself in re-touching older plays which were in the repertoire of the company to which he belonged. Among plays which the Folio editors printed as his were the Third Part of *Henry VI*, *Titus Andronicus* and the *Taming of the Shrew*, all of them re-modelled from old favourites of the stage written by other men. In the additions and embellishments which the Folio version adds to the older material we see Shakespeare's first experiments in the three patterns of History, Tragedy and Comedy. Dissimilar as his three plays are in matter and treatment, they have one striking feature in common—certain variations from the set theme handed to him which may fairly be taken as autobiographical notes, unconscious reminiscences of scenes and conditions belonging to his early life.

In September 1593, the Earl of Pembroke's company, to which Shakespeare at that time belonged, was in financial straits and, not much later, was dissolved. Their interest in the Plays which were their stock was disposed of to publishers or other companies. Among them were *Titus Andronicus*, the old *Taming of a Shrew* and a play, in the main almost certainly the work of Marlowe, generally quoted as the *True Tragedy of Richard Duke of York*, which was the foundation of the Third Part of *Henry VI*. *Titus* and the *Taming of a Shrew* were printed in quarto in 1594 and the *True Tragedy* in octavo in the following year: but the quotation from the last in Greene's *Groatsworth of Wit* shows that it was acted in 1592 or earlier. None of these plays were ascribed to Shakespeare in the titles of the early editions.

In the prototypes of the corresponding plays of the First Folio we see the crude material which Shakespeare set himself to improve before he started stage-writing on his own account. To possess the originals as well as the improved versions is an extraordinary piece of luck, which gives us a pretty clear picture of him in 'the quick forge and working-house' which within ten years produced *Hamlet* and *Lear*. At present let us note only those divergences and additions, introduced by him, which seem to have a character personal to him, and which represent

'some fragments of his dream of [early] life
Shaped by himself with newly learned art'

before London blotted out his vision of them.

But first a word as to the texture of the originals. The *True Tragedy* was acted in 1592. Marlowe died

Warwickshire Scenes in Shakespeare's Youth

in the summer of 1593. I take it that after his death the play was handed over to Shakespeare for revision, and in its altered and augmented form was printed in 1595. The *Taming of a Shrew* was printed in 1594. Shakespeare's play was acted in 1597, after the dissolution of the Pembroke men, by the united companies of the Lord Admiral and the Lord Chamberlain, to the latter of which Shakespeare had transferred himself. Shakespeare retained much of the original, touching up the Petruchio business and adding the Bianca sub-plot. More to our purpose is the circumstance that he introduced Warwickshire scenery into the Induction. In the Induction of the old play there is nothing about Barton Heath, Wincote and 'Greece.'

The case of *Titus* is more complicated. For this much-maligned drama I confess that I have a vast respect. Shakespeare was not responsible for the ghastliness of the theme, which was some other man's sop to the taste of the 'limbs of Limehouse' before they knew their Shakespeare. His contribution to it was an imaginative vigour that was absent from his original and outwent all that was reached by his predecessors in that line. In the passages which are his the flashes of description are as 'lightning in the collied night,' and—which interests me—they momentarily illuminate dark places in the writer's life.

In the shape that was given to it in the First Folio *Titus* was published in 1594, and in January of that year is mentioned by Henslowe in his diary as a new play. But in the same diary, under date April 1593, Henslowe mentions an older play, *Titus and Vespatian*, of which no English copy is extant. A play, however, called *Titus Andronicus* was performed in Germany by English actors about 1600, and one of the characters in it is called Vespatian. In an even cruder way the German version, printed by Mr Albert Cohn in his *Shakespeare in Germany*, tells the same story as the Folio play. It is not to be doubted that the latter is a re-modelling of the *Vespatian* play, which in its outlines was identical with the German *Titus Andronicus*. Strong internal evidence points to Peele as the principal author of the Folio *Titus*. In the Induction of his *Bartholomew Fair* Jonson says: 'He that will swear *Jeronimo* or *Andronicus* are the best plays yet shall pass un-excepted at here, as a man whose judgment hath stood still these five-and-twenty or thirty years.' As the date of *Bartholomew Fair* is 1614, Jonson's words, if they can be pressed into any chronological exactitude, imply that *Andronicus* was a popular play at some date between 1584 and 1589, when it is scarcely credible that Shakespeare had taken to stage-writing: nor in the body of the work is it possible to recognise the Shakespeare touch*. On the other hand, scattered through the play are passages not unworthy of the nearly contemporary *Venus*, and in some respects an anticipation of it.

---

* The writer of *Titus Andronicus* evidently had some knowledge of Greek drama: witness his allusions to the *Prometheus*, the *Hecuba* and the *Ajax*.

Warwickshire Scenes in Shakespeare's Youth

Tamora's wooing of Aaron is a blank-verse draft of the courtship of Adonis by his 'bold-faced suitor*.' Take from Shakespeare's amplified versions of the three plays some of the scenes which are not in the 'copy' before him or only faintly therein indicated. First, there is the matter of parks and chases and the 'contiguity of shade' which chequers his early, but rather later, comedies. In the Third Part of *Henry VI* there are two hunting scenes (III, 1 and IV, 5). Both have their source in the *True Tragedy*: but the talk of the keepers in the former scene is much enlarged and more keeperly in the First Folio. The scene between the Lord and the huntsmen in the Induction of the *Taming of the Shrew* is clear evidence that in the lines about the hounds (14–25) Shakespeare is drawing from his own observation: the corresponding bit of the *Taming of a Shrew* has only a faint suggestion of hunting talk. In the old play the 'Nobleman' on entering simply says to his 'men':

'Here breake we off our hunting for to night:
Cupple up the hounds, and let us hie us home:
And bid the huntsman see them meated well,
For they have all deserv'd it well to daie.'

Yet clearer is the evidence of *Titus*. With the features of classical Rome the writer shows little

* Compare Tamora, 'the babbling echo mocks the hounds, Replying shrilly to the well-tuned horns, As if a double hunt were heard at once,' with Venus, 'then do they (*i.e.* the hounds) spend their mouths: echo replies, As if another chase were in the skies'; and Tamora, 'the snake lies rolled in the cheerful sun...let us sit,' with Venus, 'here come and sit where never serpent hisses.'

more familiarity than is shown of Athens in *Mid-summer Night's Dream*. Once outside the gates of either city Shakespeare finds himself among a troop of hunting lords and ladies in an Elizabethan chase, and the 'chase' in *Titus* has a 'lodge' in it, just as the deer-parks of Shallow and the King of Navarre had, and there is talk of 'keepers,' just as there is in *Merry Wives* and *Henry VI*. Indeed, all that is said of hunting and hounds in *Midsummer Night's Dream* is but an elaboration of *Titus*, II, 2. For such sights and sounds the only hint given in the German play is the bald invitation of Titus to the Emperor, 'I have ordered a stag hunt for to-morrow' and the flat remark of Andronica's Husband, 'I can truly say that I have been at many hunts, but never did I see a gayer and merrier one.' Happenings such as Shakespeare is at un-necessary pains to describe in the three plays surely had their suggestion in things seen at some place which was denominated 'in Arden,' and not 'on Avon.'

There is another scene in *Titus* which surprises yet more by its intrusion of detail, in a double sense 'Gothic,' in a landscape proclaiming itself as Roman. Lucius, son of Titus, is encamped in some place which our editions, since Capell, describe as 'Plains near Rome': it is at least near enough to allow Lucius to accept an invitation to a parley at his father's house. To him enters a Goth, leading Aaron with a child in his arms, and delivers himself in this fashion:

Warwickshire Scenes in Shakespeare's Youth

'Renowned Lucius, from our troops I stray'd
To gaze upon a ruinous monastery;
And, as I earnestly did fix mine eye
Upon the wasted building, suddenly
I heard a child cry underneath a wall.'

There is nothing about this in the German *Titus*.
The scene, in its setting, is strange enough to
suggest that it is a picture of something familiar to
the earnest eyes of Shakespeare. Where might he
have gazed on such a ruin? At Stratford there was
no monastery, and none nearer than Alcester, eight
miles west of it: indeed southern Warwickshire was
singularly destitute of monasteries. But in Arden
there were monasteries at Atherstone, Combe,
Coventry, Maxstoke, Merevale, Nuneaton, Pinley,
Polesworth, Studley and Wroxall: also at Warwick
and Kenilworth. Any or several of these may have
been in Shakespeare's mind. But for his picture he
need not have looked farther than the ruins of
Polesworth nunnery, in the very midst of which
his youth was spent, if I am right in giving him an
upbringing in the home of the Gooderes.

In another very early play, the *Comedy of Errors*,
Shakespeare again takes us back to the monastic
surroundings of his youth. In its pseudo-classical
Ephesus there is an Abbey*, and concerning it
there is a curious descriptive note:

* 'This is some priory,' says Dromio of Syracuse, a stranger
in Ephesus: otherwise the house is always called an abbey.
Nunneries were generally priories: in Gasquet's list of English
religious houses (*English Monastic Houses*) there are, besides
Polesworth, only six abbeys.

Warwickshire Scenes in Shakespeare's Youth

'The Duke himself in person
Comes this way to the melancholy vale,
The place of death and sorry execution,
Behind the ditches of the abbey here.'

Shakespeare was not antiquarian enough to know anything about the law of *infangenethef*, which gave to certain lords, as well as monastic bodies, the right to hang thieves caught within their manorial bounds: he was probably unacquainted with the phrase, so often occurrent in charters, *furca et fossa*, a license to hang men offenders and to drown women in the manor ditch. But tradition lingered, and any old parishioner of Polesworth could point out to Shakespeare the melancholy vale and the *fossa supplicii*, and the horror of it must have possessed his young imagination, just as little Mamilius was thrilled by the tale of the man who dwelt by the churchyard.

Again, in the *Two Gentlemen of Verona*, the scene of Silvia's flight, for no apparent reason, is laid at 'Milan, an abbey,' and she directs Sir Eglamour,

'Go on, good Eglamour,
Out at the postern by the abbey wall.'

In *Midsummer Night's Dream* the Gothic features are thinly classicised. Hermia is threatened with being in 'a shady cloister mew'd' chanting hymns to the moon. Late in life Shakespeare, in *Pericles*, returned to the situation created in the *Comedy of Errors* of a husband and wife parted at sea and

116

PLATE VIII

THE ABBEY (NOW PARISH) CHURCH   POLESWORTH

brought together again after the wife has assumed 'a vestal livery' in the temple of Diana*.

For a Polesworth reminiscence of another kind, I return to Shakespeare's Induction to the *Taming of the Shrew*. In the old play there are no 'huntsmen,' and the Lord's directions as to the entertainment of Sly, given by Shakespeare rather inappropriately to the huntsmen, are addressed to the 'men.' More singular is the part assigned to the page, Bartholomew. In the old play there is no page: a boy belonging to the players' company takes the part of Sly's Lady, and it needs no Hamlet to tell us that women's parts were given to boys. So presently in the old play 'Enter the Boy in Woman's attire,' and of course nothing is said about a page's fitness for impersonating a noble lady. Why does Shakespeare give to page Bartholomew a part which in the copy before him is so very suitably given to a boy-actor? Julia, 'page' to Proteus in the *Two Gentlemen*, gives the answer when she says that in the Pentecost pageant she played the woman's part of Ariadne, 'trimmed in Madam Julia's gown.' Naturally one thinks of that 'delightful ostentation, or show, or pageant' which was presented by the

* The sisterhood of St Clare figures in *Measure for Measure*, which is one of Shakespeare's later comedies (? 1603). But Shakespeare probably got the suggestion of it from the household of the Minories in London. There were very few sisterhoods of that order in England, and none in Warwickshire. Shakespeare's recollections of Polesworth may be paralleled with Marlowe's of Canterbury. In the *Jew of Malta* (III, 4), where there is much talk of monastic matters, he mentions a 'dark entry' in a nunnery. The 'Dark Entry' in the cathedral-monastery of Christ Church is still shown.

curate and the schoolmaster to the Princess and her ladies, and in which page Moth acted as 'Hercules in minority.' In such a pageant I think it more than likely that little Will had taken a part. And it was in somebody's park, and Costard the swain was a fellow-actor, and constable Dull played the tabor or danced the hay, and altogether it was a very countrified affair. Is the apparition of Hymen in the last scene of *As You Like It* a little disconcerting? Well, there was precedent for pageant in Arden. Is there, perchance, a far-off, faint echo of pageantry and Polesworth in the cry of Postumus to the disguised Imogen?

'Shall's have a play of this? Thou scornful page,
There lie thy part!'

§ 23 THE LAST DAYS

In 1597, when Shakespeare bought the New Place, he was in the full tide of popular success. If ever he, like Scott, had dreamt of founding a family, his hopes were frustrated by the death of Hamnet in the preceding year. His motive in the purchase was to provide a home for his wife and daughters, possibly for his parents, now well advanced in years. After 1597 nothing more is heard of John's troubles or occupations. He had his quiet consummation in 1601, and his wife followed him seven years later. Besides William's wife and daughters there remained at Stratford his brother, Richard, and his sister, Joan. Pepys, who was ashamed of the rusticity of his father and sister, was yet drawn often to visit the old home at Brampton. The same ties of affection brought William to Stratford.

In 1597 he had not reached his climacteric in drama. Whether any of his later plays were planned or written at Stratford it is impossible to say. Such documents as tell us of his whereabouts between 1597 and 1611 connect him entirely with London*. The tradition noted by John Ward, vicar of Stratford, about 1662–3, that in his elder days he lived at Stratford and supplied the stage with two plays every year is, in respect of the latter statement, to be accepted with caution. After the *Tempest* (1610–11) it is likely enough that he bade farewell to the London theatre. In his last plays his invention passed beyond the bounds of Time and Space, and there is no suggestion in any of them that the scene is laid in Warwickshire surroundings.

Let Stratford content itself with the part in Shakespeare which belongs to it of right. If Polesworth is not to come into the picture, there is no other place than Stratford where we can be sure that we look on scenes once familiar to the poet. In its streets, church and museum there is all— excluding Polesworth—that is materially associated with him. It is piety, and it is good sense that directs English-speaking pilgrims thither, to recover something of the atmosphere in which the greatest

* Halliwell-Phillipps (*Outlines*, 1, p. 238) quotes evidence for thinking that Shakespeare did not make New Place his permanent residence 'until 1613 at the earliest.'

Englishman at some times breathed. There needs
no inductive process to attract the multitude to
Stratford. So it will be, and so it should be.

Nor could it be otherwise. London has no
memories of him. In the long silence of the Drama
during the Puritan captivity all vestige of his life
there was obliterated. And, apart from the un-
foreseen tyranny of the times, Shakespeare antici-
pated no other fate. To him his personality and
experiences were as the transient shadow, which,
like the poor player's presentation, signified nothing.
When Betterton awoke interest in the history of the
man, independently of his writings, the last of the
actors with whom survived any tradition of Shakespeare's playhouse days was dead: the theatres that
he had known had vanished: a new Drama had
arisen and had shifted its ground from the Bankside
to the Cockpit and Drury Lane. Betterton was
right. So far as his knowledge went, all that could
be recovered of Shakespeare's life was to be sought
at Stratford. Thither he was drawn by the famous
monument and Dugdale's picture of it—even more,
perhaps, by Jonson's undying tribute to the 'Sweet
Swan of Avon.'

Take Jonson's words as Jonson intended them.
They are a conventional classicism. The comparison
of swan and poet is as old as the Greek anthology,
and the association with local stream or spring has
its direct model in Horace:

'Multa Dircaeum levat aura cycnum,'

where the epithet means no more than that Pindar
was by birth a Theban: and for no other reason
Davenant was styled by a contemporary 'Swan of
Isis*.'

Something further, perhaps, dictated to Jonson
the swan-comparison. The lines in which it occurs
are *To the Memory of my Beloved, the Author*—an
epicedium—and he contrasts

> 'the pale, faint swan
> Who from the organ-pipe of frailty sings
> His soul and body to their lasting rest'

with the 'brave flights' in bygone days of the same
swan 'upon the banks of Thames.' Almost I am
persuaded to think that there is a likelihood of
truth in the story of that meeting—'merry' or not—
with Jonson and Drayton which preceded Shakespeare's death. It is probable enough that the
visit which Ben paid to Goodere at Polesworth was
extended to include his poetic friends at Stratford
and Clifton Chambers. Peradventure between
the three there had been talk of the past and
present doings of each of them, and, as they
mused, the fire burned, and they spoke one
to other snatches of brooded song. Of other
such meetings and of such interchange of verse
Drayton writes in his Elegy to his friend, Henry
Reynolds:

---

* A versifier of 1647 styled Samuel Daniel (a Somerset man)
'Sweetest Swan of Avon,' apparently because his 'Delia' lived
somewhere near the Bristol Avon.

The Last Days

'how oft have we,
In winter evenings, meaning to be free
To some well-chosen place used to retire,
And there with moderate meat and wine and fire
Have pass'd the time contentedly with chat,
Now talk'd of this, and then discoursed of that,
Spoke our own verses 'twixt ourselves: if not
Other men's lines which we by chance had got,
Or some stage pieces, famous long before,
Of which your happy memory had store.'

Let it stand for a guess. As I cannot but think
that Shakespeare had meditated poetry for years
before he produced the 'first heir of his invention,'
so I cannot believe that the last five years of his
life were altogether songless. What may not the
world have lost that Jonson had heard, and with
that miraculous memory of his might have repeated
for our advantage, had he cared! For undramatic
poetry the player-editors took no thought, and of
published fame Shakespeare was heedless. In the
quietude of New Place, released from the exactions
of the stage, it may well be that he devoted 'the
advantage of his idle hours' to some such 'graver
labour' as was promised in the dedication of *Venus*.
Whatever he left in writing passed with New Place
to the keeping of Susanna. Rosalind imagined for
herself an uncle-magician obscured in the circle of
Arden forest: Miranda in the enchanted island had
no eyes for wizardry. Susanna was no Rosalind.
An affectionate, pious woman, if we may judge her
character from the inscription on her monument
and that which she caused to be placed on her

122

The Last Days

mother's, she was so incapable of appreciating genius, and even of recognising familiar handwriting, that she positively denied that a book in the script of her distinguished husband, the physician, Dr Hall, was written by him. Not a soul in Stratford was at any pains to rescue the verses which Susanna devoted to lighting the domestic hearth.

CAMBRIDGE: PRINTED BY W. LEWIS, M.A., AT THE UNIVERSITY PRESS

25681931R00093

Printed in Great Britain
by Amazon